FOLKLORE & FABLES Vol. Two

AN ALTERNATIVE VIEW OF LIFE AT **BRAMALL LANE**

COMPILED BY JOHN GARRETT

EDITED BY KEVIN COOKSON

VERTICAL editions

www.verticaleditions.com

Photographs courtesy of Sheffield United's club archive

First published in the United Kingdom in 2019 by Vertical Editions, Unit 41 Regency Court, Sheffield, S35 9ZQ

www.verticaleditions.com

ISBN 978-1-908847-15-7

A CIP catalogue record for this book is available from the British Library

Cover design by Vertical Editions, Sheffield

Printed and bound by Jellyfish Print Solutions, Swanmore, Hants

This book is dedicated the beautiful memory of Jack and Audrey Garrett; without whom none of this madness would have ever occurred.

CONTENTS

Old man Garrett, John and Keith

INTRODUCTION

It doesn't seem like nearly 10 years since Kevin Cookson asked me if I could write enough words in each programme to make a regular piece. Kev had just taken over as sole programme editor at the time and was looking for new content - I had written things for the programme in the past on former players and memorabilia relating to the club that had gone down quite well. And, it must be said, I could ramble a bit!

The idea was to write an article that wasn't just about football. You can find any fact that you want these days with the click of a mouse on the internet, so it couldn't be just about stats. All matchday magazines had stuff about specific games, seasons etc, but, once again, articles had a tendency of being a bit "samey" - the challenge was to get a bit of my personal stuff and humour into the piece to add some extra relevance

My family have always featured heavily in Fables, and I can't really apologise for that. Firstly, my Dad was a lifelong fan, as was my brother. Being brought up on the Sharrow it wasn't a surprise that he and my Uncle Eric would be of the red and white persuasion. His half brother and sister, plus all of my Mum's side were of the other colours, but we tend to try and forget that - Mum saw sense when she met Dad even though she went to Hillsborough as a kid in the 1920s and 30s. It was easier that way!

I was brought up a Blade - I never knew anything different and, from the moment I was old enough to take, I was at the Lane with Pop or our kid. The fact that our Keith ran the coaches along with Dot Pearson, Alan Wright and others, also meant that I was taken from an early age to away games. And I loved every minute. The family could also, quite frequently, be a tad eccentric and also hysterically funny. I only ever really knew laughter and off-the-wall humour in our house when I was growing up, even when times were hard. For better or worse, that shaped the person that I became.

Dad had a slightly off centre way of looking at things - his favourite saying was "The more I see of the general public, the more I like dogs". Maybe not the best mantra for a newsagent, but I always got what he meant! Fables has always been a good way of linking stories about them and other situations to life, the game and, most importantly, Sheffield United FC

In over 20 years on the staff at the club, I have been fortunate to see and be involved in many happenings and landmark events around the place, meet many fascinating players, former players and people and be "on the inside" through history changing events. All these rack up in the memory bank and it's never hard to find something to talk about when you are me - as many colleagues, friends and family will doubtless testify!

The very first one we did was called "Dead Centre"- a nice, cheerful title that saw me pointing the way around the local last resting places of former greats of the Blades such as 'Fatty' Foulkes. I remember mountaineering around Burngreave Cemetery with the much-missed club photographer Martyn Harrison, to find Foulkes' his grave for a picture, me stood behind, looking suitably sombre in my Marks and Sparks rain mac, as if it was yesterday. It went down well and the rest, as they say, is history

This is the second volume of what we think are some of the best that has been produced, and it has certainly stirred a few memories as we have tried to look back through them and find what we think are some of the best done. I really hope that you, the reader, enjoy reading them as much as I did writing them.

Over the years, many things have changed that can sometimes date the article. Some people featured have sadly passed on to a higher league, transfer records for the club have been broken, but I would like to think that the very essence of why each one was written still exists when you see it again.

The article would never have been possible without Kevin Cookson. "Cooky" is as near to a brother at work as I have ever had - we started at Sheffield United back in the 1990s within weeks of each other, have lived through and seen many things here, and have probably hampered each other's careers at the Lane on many occasions over the years as well!

Fables was his idea, or at least the thought of me writing a piece for him - he has also been its editor up to the start of the 2019/20 Premier League season, having the job of correcting grammatical errors and continuity whilst also being the voice of common sense and reason when he thinks I haven't made sense or have sailed a little bit too close to the edge at times. I have always been grateful that he encouraged me to write and supported what I have written and produced - it has been his faith in me that pushed me down a road I never thought I would walk down, and made me do things I never thought I would attempt. From the start of this season, the task has fallen to another lifelong Blade who has joined the staff, Matt Young.

Club historian, Denis Clarebrough, also saw something in me many years ago and took me under his wing - I always loved and was fascinated by the history of the club and its famous home, and he was always happy (and still is) to give me much of his time, advice and anecdotes. His knowledge and enthusiasm for United and its finest detail is breathtaking.

He has one of the finest minds on football history in general that I have ever encountered and is one of life's true gentlemen to boot. It was always an accolade when he told me he had "enjoyed my ramblings" - even if he felt I hadn't got the facts quite as he saw them.

Either way, I found it the highest accolade and was just chuffed that someone I admired so much had taken time to read something that I had written. Down the years the articles have won several Programme Monthly awards as best article, and when they review our excellent Match Day programme they always say it is one of the first pieces they look for. I may have mentioned this round the offices on a few occasions over the years!

As I say, some things have changed since these Folklore and Fables were first born, but it's nice to put together another "greatest hits" so to speak, and I hope that the selection works.

Enjoy and, as ever, UTB!

John Garrett, October 2019

FOREWORD

When I joined Sheffield United Football Club from Watford nearly 20 years ago, John Garrett was one of the first people I met at the club. And here we are, all those years on and still friends. The Blades are known as 'The Family Club', and it is for a very good reason. I had been with the Hornets from being a youngster, moving up there from Wales as an apprentice - that was no small undertaking back then, swapping the Valleys for just outside of London, but the closeness there that had been fostered and nurtured from the days of Graham Taylor's first reign there made it easy. There was always an arm around your shoulder, and it meant the world.

Even as a professional footballer, to leave that was a huge decision. When Neil Warnock came in to sign me, initially on loan, I had begun to feature less and less in the first team there due to the changes brought about by the arrival of Gianluca Vialli, and, as a Wales International, I needed to be playing football. The journey up the M1 was also a big move for me and a young family but 'JG', along with many others, made it feel like home. When the chance came to put pen to paper on a permanent deal, there was no hesitation. United became my family. You will find very few football clubs of its size, history and tradition that have a backbone of staff that have worked there for 20, 25 and 30 plus years. It's unheard of and for that reason, when you have to contact them for any reason, you know exactly who to speak to and where they will be. And that means the world.

The players and the staff from that era were closely bonded. It was a great time for the club as it began to wake up and move towards what culminated in the promotion to the Premier League. I had left at that point, but the 'Triple Assault' season that saw us reach the semi- finals of both domestic cups, as well as the play-off final against Wolves, was something special. We're all pretty much in contact on a regular basis, or only a phone call away and that is the measure of the friendships that

Rob Page in his days at the Lane

were forged at that special time. John is, first and foremost, a Blade - it's the club that he grew up supporting, following his brother, Dad, and Grandad before him. It's a family thing and a way of life. He is a Blade that happens to work for the club he loves, and to him it's very special. United worked its way into my veins - it's very special to me too and, even though I have travelled the country as a player, coach and manager since, I still live in the Steel City and regard it very much as home. My eldest lad is very much a Blade and works for the academy at the club in the same way as JG's youngest works in the club shop and brother is the Referee's assistant on a match day. His eldest also worked at the club as a youngster on match days so, as I say, it's very much a family thing, which brings me to this book

Even when I was a player, JG would write things in the programme about United history , do former player interviews and other bits, but his "Folklore and Fables" section is the one that has caught the imagination of fans. If you want to find out anything about his, at times, slightly eccentric family and their life around the Lane, then this has always been the place to do so. It's the part of the programme that I always look forward to reading when I attend a game (which, living here is pretty regularly) and, it would be fair to say that no two articles are ever the same, or ever come from the same angle twice.

It always says 'let's see where his mind takes us this week' or something like that at the top of the page, and that is a fair description. It would also be fair to say that, over the years we have been friends, I have never quite worked out where his mind goes at times! He has that certain sense of humour that I think you need around a football club. He can take banter and certainly also dish it out and, believe me, that is vital when you are in and around the professional game.

This book is the second compilation of Folklore and Fables and John will occasionally will remind you that it is an 'award winning' item after taking the 'Football Monthly Article of the Year' gong on several occasions. Although he doesn't like to talk about it! I hope you enjoy reading it, as I have - it's a fascinating if slightly off-centre look at family life, football history and, of course, the Red and White Wizards.

And finally, after years of JG attacking both me and my proud Welsh heritage, I can confirm that the very blood of the valleys flows through him, as his grandfather was born and bred in Tintern before he migrated to Sheffield in the 1890s for work... something I discovered from Folklore and Fables!

Robert Page, Wales assistant manager, November 2019

CHAPTER ONE

YOUNG HEARTS...

ORIGINALLY PUBLISHED: AUGUST 16, 2016
SHEFFIELD UNITED 0 SOUTHEND 3

Remember when you were young and starting out? That time when you were making the transition from the world of school to the one that exists outside… the big wide world.

It reminded me even more when my youngest started his apprenticeship at the beginning of July. I mean, where does the time go? It doesn't seem two minutes since I proudly brought home his 'best dribbler at Bramall Lane' bib from the club shop. He made his crying, moaning debut at the Lane in his Mum's arms on 12th August 2000 at just four months old in a game we won 2-0. Paul Devlin scored and Linvoy Primus popped one in himself, for us. Very kind of him.

He was miserable all through the game; something he has, by and large, learned can be very much par for the course. I took him out onto the pitch for a photograph before the game - you know, preserve the memory of the momentous occasion and prove that, as I have suffered all my life, he was never going to be allowed to get away with it. He was so happy that, as we came off to hand him back to Mum, half a pint of Cow and Gate's finest was regurgitated all over my club blazer just before having to deal with the sponsors!

It clearly didn't work that well either; Danny came to games fairly sporadically up to around six or seven. It was then that he got the bug in a big way

Young Daniel at the Lane

and has been annoying the living daylights out of me on football and, in particular, the mighty Blades ever since.

He also developed at an early age a unique knack of being able to manoeuvre any conversation around to the red and white wizards - a truly amazing talent he has still to this day!

At the tender age of 16 he has watched SUFC on over 70 grounds. Not bad for a young 'un! My eldest is a season ticket holder and I look back with pride that both have had the illness known as Sheffield United forced onto them just as I had by their Grandad and Uncle!

I never worked out what I wanted to be when I left school, and to a certain extent I still haven't. I came onto the staff at United nearly two decades ago working in the Pools Office with Mick Rooker and have done a whole load of things since. To be honest, I have done things that I never thought I would ever get involved in - that's what football tends to throw at you. Stuff like writing, putting together the club museum, media, television and also putting together the ex-player society; that is about as diverse as it gets. No two days are ever the same and, as with children growing up, you look at the changes you have seen during your time on the staff and really wonder where the time has gone and, of course, many of the people.

I have attended far too many funerals of colleagues, fellow fans and players and always felt far worse off for knowing I would never see them again, but that's a football club, just like any family. The same events occur in its life cycle – births, deaths, and weddings etc. Just a lot more of them. I was never good enough to be a footballer, although there were plenty around at my age group who were. I was at school with Carl Bradshaw and his brother Darren, also a cracking player who made it in the league, was the year above. Schools football at that time also had the likes of John Beresford, our own manager Chris Wilder, Wayne Biggins, who was a bit older, Fraser Digby, Tony Dawes, Lee Walshaw… there were loads who went on and did fairly well for themselves at that time, with many playing for the Blades.

Back then, if my memory serves me well, they used to hold

open trials on the pitch at Bramall Lane in the summer and quite a few other clubs used to be having a sniff around for the next big thing. There were always scouts around; Chris famously got picked up by Southampton and spent his early life down there, John Beresford went to Manchester City before really making his name at Newcastle United.

That's pretty much how it went. My best mate was a Blade through and through - cut him and he bled red and white. He was also a decent, if slightly aggressive, centre half – you know the type, sent off and then back in the field of play to assault a different player with the corner flag. Anyway, despite all his efforts to seduce the eye of Cec Coldwell or John McSeveney, the only club who wanted him for a further trial was our neighbours. They sent a representative to his Hackenthorpe home. His Dad, also a Blade, said that it would be his choice. The conversation took place on the doorstep. Well, he wouldn't allow 'one of them' into the house, would he?

It made no odds. When my mate heard who was downstairs, he shut himself in the wardrobe to avoid the awkward conversation. His act of camouflage probably robbed him of his only chance to be a player and Hillsborough will sadly never know the joys of seeing an opponent flattened with a corner flag. Their loss, I say!

Towards the end of last season, a fan dropped by a great picture taken around 1963-64 of our youth team, all full of that same hope and ambition that we touched on earlier. The thing with these sorts of pictures is that the faces are not always the easiest to put names to, the same as today; these boys were the cream of the local crop at a time when our track record of picking the very best up under Archie Clark was second to none. And yet no-one adds the names below.

Taken in front of the old John Street Stand and resplendent in their v-neck Bukta shirts, they look a motley crew. I haven't really seen Len Badger over the summer to pick his brains as he knows everyone from that era, but straight away I spotted a very young Geoff Salmons on the front row, second from the left. Also, because I knew him and on the same row but third from the right, I also immediately got Phil Cliff. He went on to do a bit with us as well as Chesterfield.

Geoff certainly did OK for himself and I would like to know what his secret is – apart from the 'tache he never seems to age at all. Must be something in the water out Rotherham way.

The picture is a young set of lads setting out on a journey. As we all know, sometimes the road doesn't always take us the way we want or expect. I wonder what they all felt the day that snap was taken, where they wanted to get to and how they were going to do it.

I hope that they all got somewhere they needed to be, whether it was in football or elsewhere. It's still a great picture.

CHAPTER TWO

PERMANENT FIXTURES

ORIGINALLY PUBLISHED: AUGUST 22, 2016
SHEFFIELD UNITED 2 BLACKPOOL 0

Of course, it is not the football season but there is a day in June that we all look forward to.

It is the day that planning can start to release you from gardening, Meadowhall, taking kids to ballet and visiting family members that you avoid for the rest of the year. Yes, I'm referring to the day the fixtures come out.

Fans sit waiting for them to hit the internet. Where will you kick off, where will it end and what will be the position you, as a club, are in on that day? Also, the realisation that you actually are playing Blackpool away on a Tuesday night in December and not a hot August day, and that most of the really good games that set the pulses racing will be switched to a Friday evening or Sunday lunchtime for television purposes.

Away games are scrutinised; I know from experience that they are lovingly planned. Where will you stop, who will you travel with, and how will you get there? Also the subject of which pub has the best of beers and food on offer, but keep that one quiet!

If you work in football it means something different again. You look straight away at what the Boxing Day fixture is and, more to the point, where it is being played. Same with the New Year offering. Being at work on that June day sees the phone go into meltdown. Matchball sponsorships, mascot packages and season ticket renewals, because you can smell the start of the new campaign. Then there is your personal diary; how your life fits around the game and vice versa. There can be some fairly terse looks when and where football fixtures and family

events are concerned. I mean, when has a silver wedding anniversary ever been more important than Burton Albion away,
for pity's sake? I mean, we may never ever play there again in
a league or cup game and then the opportunity is well and
truly missed. With a bit of luck those concerned may live to see
the golden one and then there is even more to celebrate, isn't
there?

I have the new experience this time around of missing a
home and away scenario due to being the best man at a wedding. For some reason other mates have avoided involving me
like the plague where nuptials are concerned. I cannot for the
life of me think why. I mean, I am known for being shy, retiring and incapable of arranging someone being handcuffed to a
Smurf for the duration of the stag do. Honestly!

The advent of better communication has improved no end
over the years, hasn't it? As I go sight-seeing and brass rubbing
in Prague this September we will be playing Colchester United
at home. You can bet that I will be kicking every ball and be in
touch throughout the match.

In the past I have been a guest at a wedding in the city that
has started at 11am and then seen the entire male contingent,
including groom, take their places on the terraces at kick-off
time at the Lane – that in itself wasn't too bad, but the session at Silks after, instead of heading to his own reception, was
probably a move too far!

Birth is another issue that will cross paths with the average
footy fan as time goes on. The arrival of another Junior Blade on
the scene will mean the need to be present in the delivery suite.
Now, there is a fair chance that family planning will never quite
match with a fixture at Yeovil, I can testify to this from personal
experiences. My youngest arrived on 1st April 2000. A birthday
that is one of the easiest to remember, though he is anything
but an April fool and has made a top Blade himself.

That was a Sunday and we were away that day at Ewood
Park for a tasty fixture against Blackburn Rovers. All were a little
bemused as I picked updates up via my brick of a Nokia at the
Northern General – it was a welcome to the world that sets

Jamie Ward celebrates his winner against Preston

out your life as a Blade. We got whacked 5-0 – welcome to the world, son.

Death, finally, will play a part. How many generations have gone before? How many fans, how many players? How many colleagues?

My mum's last months were hard. I will never forget being on the pitch with the mascots for the game against Preston North End – 28th December 2009. We were just getting ready to get down in the tunnel to lead the teams out when her neighbour phoned me to let me know she had taken a turn for the worse. I finished off, sorted the kids out and drove back to Handsworth, phoning the paramedics in between. Mum pulled through and Jamie Ward scored the winner in a 1-0 victory. Not a bad day, that one.

The final journey of many a Blade has been to be laid under the pitch, the last wish of many - to be placed where they felt they belonged, under the turf at Bramall Lane, forever supporting.

The new Desso pitch now in operation means that, because of the way it is constructed, we will no longer be able to lay those who have passed to a higher league under the famous surface. You just can't dig into it, as simple as that. We are already looking at alternatives, ones that are in keeping with reflecting that life, that love and that loyalty. Fitting, right and proper.

Where will we be by the time that we play Scunthorpe United at the end of May?

All of the above will have gone on amongst the extended Blades family over the period that begins in earnest today. Many things in our lives will change... birth, marriage, divorce, job changes, house moves and everything else that goes on. One of the few that stays constant from the cradle to the grave is the football club that you support.

That really is a permanent fixture.

CHAPTER THREE

JUST THE TICKET

ORIGINALLY PUBLISHED: SEPTEMBER 27, 2014
SHEFFIELD UNITED 2 GILLINGHAM 1

It's amazing what people collect, isn't it? Some stuff makes perfect sense and some really does question sanity. Football collectables come into both categories, for me.

Like a lot of kids, I started out with footy programmes as you would probably expect. In fact the root of my obsession, with all things Blades and historical, comes from the programmes and bits and bobs handed down our side of the family from my Grandad . He was born in Tintern in Wales way back in 1858, moving to Sheffield to work for Viners in the early 1890s and watching us in the days when we took our fledgling steps in the Football League.

I still have a selection of late 1890s programmes that were his and they are beautiful things, well written and also featuring photographs way back when. Advanced to say the least. And I am sure that the tales of Foulkes and Co. sowed the seeds for my issues in later life – thanks Grandad! Records, music ones, were another hobby. I used to hunt high and low at flea markets, jumble sales and, of course, Violet Mays on Matilda Street in the legendary pound bin for rarities and original pressings. In fact I became quite good at it and bought (and sold) some real peaches down the years.

Coincidentally, the building that many remember as Violet Mays was also, in a previous life, the shop owned in town by the legendary Fatty Foulkes and his family. Concert tickets were the next. I love my music, as anyone who knows me will tell you. You know how old you are when your kids get into your music and I have been lucky to see some top stuff down the

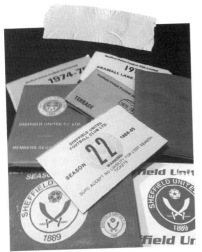

Some of JG's old tickets...

years. I have also kept a ticket stub for most of them, and they seem to be getting really sought after these days. Someone offered me £30 for a stub for The Jam at the Top Rank Suite on the Trans Global Express Tour in 1982 - to see the band cost £3.50.

It just goes to show that you should always hang on to stuff as one man's rubbish... Our school band at City was Pulp, and back in the day there were three of them – Jarvis Cocker, Jim Sellars on drums and Jamie Pinchbeck on bass. I still have a ticket for one of their first gigs which took place in the school hall one lunch time. Pulp were always brilliant and Jarvis a true character. I wonder how much that one is worth?!

Blades tickets were the same. Coming from a family of season ticket holders there was never the game to game ones, but most of the old books have been kept. The real trophy here, as far as I was concerned, was for the aways, and the story here is very much the same. So many got thrown away that there are less and less of them around, and I even forget what I have got and why, at times.

One of the first games I was ever taken to as a nipper is a bit of a blur for many reasons, the main one being that I was terrified, mainly down to the amount of people there, and for many reasons it has gone down as a game with a fair bit of fame attached to it. That game was on Saturday 2nd October 1972 and it was courtesy of a trip with Dad over the Pennines to the Theatre of Dreams then more resembling a theatre of rust known as Old Trafford – home of Manchester United.

Old Trafford has a massive part to play in SUFC history. We have played a fair few FA Cup semis there as well as the final itself in 1915, so it's not as though we were strangers across there.

The reason for the visit was very simple; after a fine promotion season the one before playing some top class football. We sat pretty at the top of what we now know as the Premier League and that, in the eyes of father, was something to be very proud of indeed.

We took the car over and I can't remember where we got parked, all I can feel still is the sheer volume of people trying to get up to the stadium. Dad lifted me onto his shoulders so I didn't get stood on, or lost. I couldn't see anything as he was technically a Hobbit. I think at 5ft 8in I am the tallest Garrett by far, or at least at the moment.

Len Badger told me that there were so many trying to get to the ground that the team had to alight from the coach about a mile or so from the ground. At that point, mixed in with fans of both clubs, Woodward, Currie, Colquhoun, Salmons and all had to unload the huge wicker baskets full of kit and boots off and carry the damned things there. Imagine that today! Roads and links around most grounds have improved beyond belief, especially around Old Trafford, which is unrecognisable today. But top flight players and internationals aplenty lugging the stuff there? Incredible.

We sat in the Railway End and I can't remember a thing about the match, it just happens to be one of those games that, over 40 years later, never seems to go away. It was a lock out, none of the "no ticket – no admission" that we know today, although we did have them for the seats, row six, 113 and 114 just for the sake of the record! It was a lock out, ground full and thousands of supporters from both clubs left outside the ground, and the noise inside was the only thing I am clear about.

Manchester United won the game 2-0 and it will always be famed for the George Best goal that still gets milked more than a dairy herd today. You will have seen it; Len Badger does every time he closes his eyes, as it is he who ends up on his backside in the net valiantly trying to clear the goal-bound effort from one of the true greats of the game.

My elder brother, who had gone across in his Ford Corsair,

returned to find it had gone, along with a week's takings from one of our newsagent shops at Commonside. So a bad day all round… especially when it came to explaining it to Dad.

Not a bad 'un for my first away day, though, and there would be many more with both big brother and Dad as I started getting dragged into it more and more.

Mum once asked him why he was taking me as he dragged me out one cold, wet night to see a game against Barnsley that was a County Cup semi final – we won 2-0 and John Flynn and 'TC' scored in front of a tiny Lane crowd.

He simply replied: "I have suffered all of my life, he is not getting away with it."

And I'm glad he did.

CHAPTER FOUR

THE SABELLA DOCUMENTS

ORIGINALLY PUBLISHED: AUGUST 9, 2014
SHEFFIELD UNITED 1 BRISTOL CITY 2
AND DECEMBER 28, 2014
SHEFFIELD UNITED V SCUNTHORPE (POSTPONED)

I never went abroad until my late teens with the lads. My Dad said he had spent five years there during the war and people had kept trying to kill him… that had put him off slightly.

I learned very quickly that there were a few important differences, the most important probably being that if you gave any of the police there some lip they tended to all turn up wearing Ray Bans and carrying guns. Maybe things hadn't changed too much from when Dad was there, then! As a young Sheffield lad it was a case of finding out where you could get a full English breakfast at two in the afternoon and also where the The Sun was available back then. In my opinion it had the best political slant and viewpoint… honest it did!

There were other things that were new and coming from Sheffield, the sun was a novelty for a start. The first year I went to Ibiza, and summer in Yorkshire had been on a Thursday afternoon at two o'clock. The next was the ability to hire a Honda 50 and drive round the Old Town like a maniac with no helmet on and three mates on the back. This worked well until coming off it and lodging it under a tour bus. How the hire company laughed as we carried it back in and tried to run off – the next important lesson was never leave your passport with a hire company. You live and learn.

Ibiza also meant a re-education as to diet and culinary culture and cuisine; ripe Mediterranean tomatoes, fresh locally caught fish and salad produce. We had none of that. I had foreseen

Alex Sabella was a Blade

trouble and, on Mum's advice, I took plenty of Pot Noodles and Monster Munch!

Toilet seats were also different. Mum had warned me about those as well, so most of the ones that I saw were mummified in toilet roll. I mean, you could catch anything from one, Mum said so! Finally, language. Ibiza wasn't deepest darkest Peru, but Spanish wasn't English. In fairness and in certain situations hand gestures tend to bridge all cultures, just go back to my comment regarding the Police!

Now, I have never really lived anywhere other than the Steel City. Moving from Hackenthorpe to Handsworth was more than enough, I mean, how many of your possessions can you cram into a transit van after dark without alerting the neighbours?

If that was the case then what must it have been like to move halfway around the world to work? A few weeks ago we were tidying out a few of the old store cupboards when I found a set of files regarding Alex Sabella joining us from River Plate in 1978.

The first thing that really struck me was the amount of red tape that we had to go through back then. For a start the club had to petition the Department of Employment to get their permission, then there was a whole pile of stuff between the clubs – their President, Rafael Aragon Cabrera, agreed the fee of 275,000 United States dollars to be paid to them over a period of 120 days – still a hell of a sum back then.

As soon as he passed to this country as an employee he got a National Insurance number and away we went. We had got him a house at Thorpe Drive in Waterthorpe in the south east of the city, so all good there, but I had never even given a thought to the fact that a house would need furniture!

The Football League were involved, somehow, and we had to get a quote to ship the lot over here from SB Hogg (Removals) Limited of Burngreave. Apparently, to bring his stuff over back then would have a cost attached of £1,900 to be paid for by the club. Once they were here they would then be classed as the property of Sheffield United FC! A lot of money for a Hoover, twin tub washer, a black and white Ferguson 20 inch TV and an old pouffe, don't you think?

Incidentally, the house was bought with a mortgage from the Burnley Building Society and he had to sign an agreement with them that was countersigned by United - agreeing that, in the event of his leaving the country and heading back to the land of pampas and polo, we would repay any outstanding balance.

Upon his signing, he got a weekly basic wage of £110 per week plus appearance, win and points bonuses, so he would have little problem there in meeting dues and demands there I would have thought. He and the club would have been glad that he had found a home – up to that point he and his wife had been resident in the St. George's Hotel at Kenwood Park, not far from the ground... at the club's expense!

United bit the bullet and bought new. Alex needed the lot right down to an iron (£7.50), tableware at £26.42 and some net curtains with which to twitch. Do you think that Eden Hazard asked for some nets when he joined Chelsea? They would look good on a mock Tudor in Esher wouldn't they? The future manager of Argentina also needed a cleaner. No, not the type who comes in twice a week with a back door key but one that you change the bag on and plug in. Oh, the glamour of it all in '78.

It all combined to a bill of £2,285.77 of the Queens realm. Eye-watering stuff and clearly the best stuff that money could buy, all signed off by United secretary Dick Chester to keep the Sabellas happy in their new home.

Gilders, the car people from the city, had also got the lad on the move and given him a Volkswagen Scirocco, proper car that back then. That was all good, but it seems as though our Alex hadn't quite got the hang of the parking laws of this country because the company had also invoiced United for two tickets issued to him by South Yorkshire's finest. One of them came in town on Cambridge Street, and both of them added up to £16.50. I have a family connection with parking fines and a Sheffield first by the way, my late father was the first man in the city to appear in court charged with feeding parking meters with foreign coins. He would have had a few handed over to him no doubt as he owned a shop... he pointed out that they all looked the same and it wasn't his fault that the meters accepted them!

He must have been convincing because they let him off with it. That was back in 1967, so he obviously didn't get them off señor Sabella, who did not arrive on these shores for another 11 years!

He went on to join a select band of former Blades to have taken part in World Cups. How many have done so? I suspect the best of us will miss out a few here.

Ted Burgin may have been the first, and as far as I know Ted is still well and living in Blackpool. Alan Hodgkinson definitely was a part of two World Cup squads back in the day of Walter Winterbottom and Len Badger was, I believe, part of Sir Alf Ramsey's 1966 World Cup shadow squad. Keith Kettleborough was on standby, although he may have been a Newcastle United player by that time.

Of course, Martin Peters famously lifted the Jules Rimet Trophy in 1966 but was a West Ham player back then. Hammers occasionally point out that they virtually won the World Cup, and with three players all making major contributions, who can argue? Martin's career here at Bramall Lane ended any further involvement in the game. A player ten years ahead of his time on the pitch but the wrong man at the wrong time for an ailing Sheffield United – he made mistakes but took the can for the failings of others over a number of years.

Alan Kelly travelled to the USA with the Republic of Ireland in 1994 and Roger Nilsen was a squad member of Norway's contingent the same year, and I suppose there are a fair few others

SHEFFIELD UNITED
FOOTBALL CLUB LIMITED

REGISTERED OFFICES AND GROUND: BRAMALL LANE, SHEFFIELD S2 4SU.
ENGLAND REG. No. 61564
TELEGRAMS: 'UNITED, SHEFFIELD. TELEPHONE: 738955/6/7

COLOURS: RED AND WHITE STRIPES
MANAGER:
SECRETARY: K. WALKER

INTERNATIONAL TRANSFER AGREEMENT

Between the RIVER PLATE ATHLETIC CLUB, represented herein by Mr. RAFAEL ARAGON CABRERA, President and the SHEFFIELD UNITED FOOTBALL CLUB LIMITED of Sheffield, England, represented herein by Mr. HARRY HASLAM, Manager, the following is hereby agreed: - - - - - - - -

FIRSTLY: The RIVER PLATE ATHLETIC CLUB cedes to the SHEFFIELD UNITED FOOTBALL CLUB LIMITED all rights held over its player ALEJANDRO SA-BELLA, for the sum of U$S 275.000 (TWO HUNDRED AND SEVENTY FIVE THOU-SAND AMERICAN DOLLARS), to be paid in the following manner: - - - - On signing the present agreement: U$S 30.000 (THIRTY THOUSAND AMERI-CAN DOLLARS) - On the satisfactory finalization of the medical examination: ////// U$S 125.000 (ONE HUNDRED AND TWENTY FIVE THOUSAND AMERICAN DOLLARS)- At 60 days: U$S 60.000 (SIXTY THOUSAND AMERICAN DOLLARS) - - - - - - At 120 days: U$S 60.000 (SIXTY THOUSAND AMERICAN DOLLARS) - - - - -

SECONDLY: All expenses incurred in this transfer will be met by the RIVER PLATE ATHLETIC CLUB -

THIRDLY: The RIVER PLATE ATHLETIC CLUB must play 1 (one) match with SHEFFIELD UNITED FOOTBALL CLUB LIMITED, for which the SHEFFIELD /// UNITED FOOTBALL CLUB LIMITED will pay the sum of U$S 30.000 (THIRTY THOUSAND AMERICAN DOLLARS). The date of the said match is to be // arranged by mutual agreement of the two parties.- - - - - - - - - -

FOURTH: This transfer is subject and conditional on a satisfactory medical examination of the player taking place and a work permit /// being made available.- -

By mutual agreement, two copies of this document are hereby signed this day the eighteenth of July, Nineteen Seventy Eight.- - - - - -

(handwritten margin notes:)
PAID 26/7/78
PAID 26/8/78
PAID 25/9/78
DUE 21/1/79
PAID 30/9/78

HARRY HASLAM
SHEFFIELD UNITED F.C. LTD.

RAFAEL ARAGON CABRERA
RIVER PLATE ATHLETIC CLUB

RIVER PLATE   7821332
Home   41/2144
office   49/7183

The international transfer agreement for Sabella's services

that will have done it before or after passing down the Cherry Street car park. I am not really trying to put together the definitive list here, that is best done over a beer isn't it?

We have had former players and managers involved in international set ups over the years – Joe Mercer had a spell in charge of England between custodians and, of course, Ray Lewington had an excellent season in the red and white in the mid 1980s before an inability to settle sent him back down south. For those who don't know, Ray is Roy Hodgson's right hand man.

I love the World Cup. Once every four years it is a great bridge between what really matters – the Blades and the Football League. All didn't go well for England - that tends to be an all too familiar phrase - so, after the usual early journey home, who do you end up wanting to win it?

Brazil? Germany? Holland? There was only one choice for me... Argentina. The reason should be obvious... their manager was, of course, Sabella.

For my age group, Alex offered the ultimate in dreams and his arrival coincided with the change over from going to the game with Dad to going with mates in the Imma pen.

The Imma pen – what a place that was. For the uneducated, this was the crumbling triangle that sat between the John Street stand and the Kop, and a designated area for all those of a similar age and mentality (young and daft) to stand together and watch the game as big lads and lasses – only to be picked up by your Mum or Dad outside!

Sabella changed the club. He made us quite sexy again in the eyes of the watching football world. Sheffield United had been off the radar and on the slide for a couple of years and suddenly we explode into the country that has just staged and won the World Cup to sign a player – not any player, the first of his kind in the English game and once again a first for the Blades.

Of course, we could have had Diego Maradona. That's true and not a fable, and is covered in many a book and article that has been written. We could have saved England many an embarrassing moment had we let him loose in a League Cup tie on

NATIONAL INSURANCE NUMBER CARD

Please show this number to your employer, if he asks for it, and quote it in all communications with DHSS (see Notes overleaf).

Your National Insurance number is:

MR/~~MRS/MISS~~* ALEJANDRO   FORENAME(S)

SABELLA   SURNAME

THORPE DRIVE   FULL POSTAL

WATERTHORPE   ADDRESS

SHEFFIELD Postcode S19 6HU.

*Delete as appropriate

Issued by the Department of Health and Social Security

Form CF 354

a cold Tuesday night in the mud of The Shay or Sincil Bank, but, of course, it wasn't to be.

Sabella was a new dawn for all, the first player to hang your hat or shirt on since TC had departed up the M1, and boy did we sign up for it. The problem was that Sabella was a yard and a half ahead of most of the other players out on the park and boy did he look out of place, with his socks rolled down - trying hard to dance as some Third Division defender tried hard to remove his ankles from the rest of his body.

Along with Alex came the merchandise – I still proudly own my Sabella scarf (signed I hasten to add) along with a variety of button badges boasting such legends as 'Allez Les Rouges' and 'Sabella Strikes Faster Than Leyland'. It sold from the little old club shop from the corner of John Street by the box load – this was possibly the start of the modern phenomena of the souvenir.

How bizarre then, as a Blade, to see him on the touchline managing the national side, with the caption of 'Alejandro Sabella'. We have tried to bring him back before, when we played the pre-season game against Estudiantes and he was coach, but at that point he was locked in talks with the AFA and couldn't come. That said, in any interview he talked warmly of United and Bramall Lane.

It has to be said that his presence gave us plenty of name checks all over the world. It was remarkable that, as they progressed in the tournament, the penny dropped and we were inundated with requests for his number from the media. Of course, we always hand out the telephone number of the Argentina manager, don't we?! The best one was a request to speak to his former manager, the late Harry Haslam. Now that was a tough one and Derek Acorah was busy at the time! At least Tony Kenworthy was pleased to oblige with bids to talk to teammates and he did it in style.

Sabella wasn't the easiest of former players to recognise either, was he? The older Alex looked a bit like a bloke who sits in the corner of the Cross Keys at the weekend reading the Express didn't he? That said, here was one of my childhood idols managing a team in a World Cup final, and I loved it! For once I had a reason to get into the final and actually connect, although ultimately the best team did win.

Just think, there is someone living in a house in Mosborough that once belonged to the manager of a team in a World Cup final!

CHAPTER FIVE

HANGING WITH WILL.I.AM

ORIGINALLY PUBLISHED: MARCH 28, 2015
SHEFFIELD UNITED 1 CREWE ALEXANDRA 2

My Match of the Day appearance, and hanging with Will.i.am. Now that's a headline I never thought I would write! But both are true and were the result of me representing Sheffield United on the beautiful Mediterranean island of Malta. If that hasn't got your attention then nothing will, so here's the meat on the bones, so to speak...

You will remember our sponsorship deal with Malta from a few years ago - that was a first, a club sponsored by a country and many friends were made which remain today. As part of the deal and to coincide with the first team spending a pre-season training camp there, we had also agreed to take our 'Fit for School' project over to educate locals about Sheffield United and our city's links with the beautiful game.

My colleague, Dave McCarthy, had been over there for a few weeks setting everything up – pitches, venues, hotels, transfers and travels, all needed to take the Blades on the road. I was going out there partly in my role as player liaison officer, as we had hospital and school visits planned, partly to curate the museum display and to lend a hand on a few of the fan-based events that Dave had put in place.

The cabin crew clearly thought I was someone else. There was nothing too much trouble for them; half bottle of red, meal, teddy bear dressed as an airline pilot, the works. I just kept getting worried about the size of the bill when they realised I was John Garrett and not James Beattie! Fortunately, nearly a decade on, I still haven't seen the bill!

Everything there was superb on that pre-season trip of a few years ago. The Maltese people are different class and the place is stunning.

The trip saw us stationed in the Excelsior Hotel and a busy diary of events was underway. The venue for the exhibition was stunning; one of the bases for the Knights Templar, a very old building, all marble pillars and floors. We took our FA Cup replica, winners' medals, shirts, caps and the original handwritten rules of football, which were then the property of their authors, Sheffield FC, and sold later for in excess of £1million – valuable paperwork to say the least. We also took the first ever football trophy, the Youdan Cup, and you can imagine that we had quite a number of talking points for the Maltese natives, who are all football-mad.

As part of the exhibition, there was a fair bit of publicity to do with the local media organisations and I was invited to appear on the Maltese equivalent of 'Match of the Day', called 'Kick Off', I wasn't going to turn that down, was I? Many will recall that back then, on our books, we had the Maltese international goalkeeper, Justin Haber, a lovely lad and a legend out there. His missus presented 'Kick Off' and they were like the Posh and Becks of Malta!

Raquel (Posh, to Justin's Becks) was a lovely lass and we were in make up together before the show – me in make up, never needed it before! My appearance on 'Kick Off' was supposed to be about our museum collection and the first question I got asked was about that day's sacking of Tony Adams! I don't know how the Maltese viewers took my expert analysis of Portsmouth's dismissal of the former Arsenal and England defender, but I didn't get an invite to be a regular pundit on the show!

Also on the trip, I found out that Justin had a considerable collection of tropical fish and he kept them in a house left to him when his Nan died. Once a proud and hard-working family lived there, now it was tanks full of darting colours! Justin had taken myself and Andy Daykin to see his fishy friends. They all had names as well, I kid you not! They were like family, almost like going back to 'school' (get it?)

When he opened the downstairs apartment door our faces

Justin Haber. left - Dave McCarthy hands out t-shirts in Malta

were bathed in an eerie light – the glow from the tanks made it look like something from Close Encounters. Rows and rows of them. What also became quite apparent very quickly was the fact that Justin had a name for each one of his prized possessions. He took great pride in telling us how much each one had cost; and they weren't cheap, I can tell you. Clearly, he had a bond with aquatics, although I don't think he appreciated us christening him 'Fish Fingers' – nothing to do with his goalkeeping skills, I can assure you!

I swear that, to our hysterics, he introduced us to one called 'Morgs' – he told me it was because it was a fighting fish that dominated the tank and had the skipper's qualities – I pointed out that it was he who would need them if Morgs found out he had a fish named after him!

It didn't really work for Justin here, but he is still playing out there in the top-flight, has a squillion international caps, a soccer school and is still followed everywhere in Malta by a load of adoring fans.

I can honestly say, that night, he 'scaled' new heights and was never 'out of his depth'. He was a 'dab' hand at looking after them and he wasn't out of 'plaice'. OK, I will give up now. Unfortunately, Justin didn't play for us many times so we couldn't judge how good he was in the 'net'!

Back at the hotel, I was introduced to Justin's family. His Mum and Dad were lovely and so proud of their boy and quite rightly so. I was also given the pleasure of meeting his sister, and I had to take a double take on her name. This Maltese beauty had been bestowed with the name Pearl.

Now, you have to take into account the pronunciation of Haber in Malta is 'Harbour'. Yup, she was named after the battle that brought America into the thick of WWII, though I suspect that they didn't twig the significance. Pearl Haber. Brilliant. As well as the 'Fit For School' project, promoting the club, my TV appearance and the players preparing for the new season, our trip also coincided with a major music festival – Isle of MTV – and we were given free tickets by the organisers.

Set in a church square just outside the Valletta walls, it was huge gig. Lady Gaga and the Black Eyed Peas were performing and our players and staff were invited into the Cisk Lager VIP area, overlooking the stage. Not really my cup of tea (it didn't have Paul Weller there), but nice anyway and an experience I will never forget. The players had to go straight back to the hotel at the end of the performances, due to the heat, plus they were training first thing next morning, but I had a few hours off so accepted a kind invitation to the after show party. Why not indeed!

I breezed past all security and into the place where the beautiful people were at the side of the pool, they had even created an artificial beach, complete with huts and the full works. I relieved a waiter of a couple of cold beers and began to enjoy the proceedings. Perching on a wall to rest one of the beers, a guy sat down next to me and began to have a natter.

Of course I recognised him; Will.i.am. Even I knew that he was the creative force behind the Black Eyed Peas, and very pleasant he was too. He asked me who I was. I told him. He had never heard of me.

He asked me who I worked for. I told him Sheffield United. He asked me who they were.

He asked me where I was from. I told him Handsworth. He hadn't heard of that either. Clearly he needed to do a little homework.

He told me that he knew David Beckham. I told him that I didn't as he wasn't a Blade and he didn't come from Handsworth.

Joking aside, he was nice to talk to and I was invited down onto the private beach where I met his band-mate, Fergie. The things I do for this football club! I'd love to tell you we exchanged numbers and hang out when we get a chance, but we didn't and I bet he can't remember me or probably that night full stop.

United takes you to some funny situations and places at times. Malta was one of those times I will never forget, even though there was something fishy about Justin Haber!

Johnny Ertl and Chris Morgan with a young fan in Malta

CHAPTER SIX

WOODY OR WOULDN'T HE?

ORIGINALLY PUBLISHED: MARCH 7, 2015
SHEFFIELD UNITED 1 FLEETWOOD TOWN 2

Let's face facts, we don't see enough of Alan Woodward around Bramall Lane do we? There is, of course, a very good reason for that in so much as he lives in Tulsa and not at High Green. Our greatest post-war goalscorer moved there 35 years ago to play for the Roughnecks in the old Soccer League out there. In fact many Blades did and our former secretary, the late Keith Walker, went out there to do a similar job for them.

Eddie Colquhoun also went. Keith Eddy and Ken Furphy left S2 to join the New York Cosmos and a player called Pele, it always makes me smile when the greatest player ever scores a goal for the New York side and you then see him get hugged by another former Blade in the shape of Tony Field!

'Woody' was one of one my first football heroes, and I think it was for a variety of reasons… The hair, prematurely a shock of grey, even with my limited knowledge of the game at five-years-old, wherever he was on the pitch I could see where he was, he stuck out a mile!

The 'Head for Housley's' sign that was on the front of the Bramall Lane stand and just along from the supporters' club clock featured his head, or at least a caricature of it, and that was there for a good period of time after he left. I had a 'Woody' pennant on my bedroom wall, it told me 'Sheffield United are Magic' and I was quite in agreement. He bridges the gap between hazy childhood memories of games with my Dad and those colour ones of going in the Kop pen with my mates. In later life his son Shaun and I also became mates, long before I darkened the door of Bramall Lane as a member of staff. As young 'uns we worked for the same firm and got on well from the moment that we met. We were both big Blades - well, you would expect Shaun to be I suppose with a Dad like that. Thing was, he never told me who his Dad was – I swear that it took him six months to reveal. Wasn't exactly Poirot though, was I? The surname should have hinted, that and the fact that son is the spitting image of Dad and also fairly snowy in the hair department! We used to have a right old laugh battering the opposition followers with our banter and ours is a friendship that has lasted some 30 years, so all good there.

'Woody' wasn't well a few years ago and that is an under-statement to say the least. The 125 dinner a few months ago meant that we wanted to get him home, and he wanted to come. A few meetings and the job was done, flights booked, and a legend landed back in Blighty the day before the big celebration. I hadn't seen him in nearly a decade as his last visit was a fleeting one to attend a family funeral. This time was for a better reason and there was no way that he wouldn't have been here, and quite right too.

When someone doesn't get back often it means that the number of people wanting to shake your hand and say hello is crazy. On the Friday afternoon in the hotel and on the Saturday morning it was mad. Former players, employees, family mem-bers and fans all popped in to see him and welcome him back to BDTBL – more than a few autograph hunters as well, and they really are a breed all of their own.

Anyway, after the mayhem of the 125 dinner and other as-sociated dates, the calm set in over Bramall Lane once more. Woody had his diary full with meetings with family and friends, along with his travelling partner and local bar owner from across the pond, Corey, so all was well. A meeting later in the week told us he was at a loose end on Friday night, it was a lucky loose end as well. I was out for a few beers with a mate for his birthday not far from the hotel, did he want to hook up? Yes, that would be fine, so a meeting time was agreed in the Cop-thorne and away we went.

Now, I like a good pint of real ale, and, to be fair, Sheffield

Alan Woodward came back over for the 125 dinner

isn't a bad place to do it in. There are a great many good places to indulge in this hobby in the Steel City, and we headed for the meeting point a short ride away. Good pubs should be wrapped in cotton wool, shouldn't they? You know, proper Sheffield ones where there is little or no piped music and an atmosphere full of good conversation. What better place than to catch up with a real United legend? Special company indeed and a rare opportunity. Once the tipple had been chosen our group sat down for a chin wag.

It's not hard to spot 'Woody' still - the hair gives the game away from a distance in a pub in the same way that it did for me on a football pitch all those years ago. I knew a few who were in there, including a fair number of the dark side of the city's supporters, but good lads all the same. Greetings and handshakes were offered and introductions made as an Owl worked his way round the group. "And this is Alan," was the last gambit. He looked at him. He looked again. "Is that Alan Woodward?" I nodded in the affirmative. "THE Alan Woodward?" Again I confirmed the answer to his question. He leaned over and shook his hand.

"Listen, I can't stand you lot, I'm a season ticket holder at Hillsborough, but you are a proper legend. My Dad won't believe that I have met you. What an honour, a proper player. Would you have a picture taken with me?"

"No problem," was the reply, and 'Woody' duly obliged to a thrilled member of the blue side. It went down well as a fair few of his like-minded mates also approached and also, showing the maximum respect, asked for the same. He also told one of them that he could have signed for Wednesday before us, but he didn't like Vic Buckingham as he had the remains of his dinner down his tie and jacket when he went to meet him with his parents at Hillsborough. It was the friendly nature of the club and John Harris's nice car that swung the deal for the Blades. Well done gentleman John!

All had a great night; 'Woody' was quite the celebrity, and rightly so. As one of the Wednesday lads said, 'A proper player'. That was probably an understatement, but it just shows that, no matter what your allegiances, quality always shines across the great divide. Legend? More like one of the very best!

CHAPTER SEVEN

DRIVEN TO IT!

FIRST PUBLISHED: OCTOBER 21, 2014
SHEFFIELD UNITED 2 YEOVIL TOWN 0

The 125 anniversary dinner last month was one of those rare occasions when, as a Blade, you know you will never do anything quite like it again. So many heroes gathered under one roof at one time, real red and white heaven. And it is always a bonus when they live up to expectations, isn't it? One of the best things I have ever had the pleasure of being involved in, in a professional capacity, was the presentation of Eddie Colquhoun's Scottish cap – the moment was truly priceless and you felt actually privileged to have been in the room at the same time.

Eddie had mentioned a few years ago that you were only given a cap north of the border if you played in all of the Home internationals that season. Eddie had been judged good enough to have lined up against such International forces as Holland and Brazil, so he missed out because he had not played against England and the likes – amazing isn't it? Anyway, a couple of phone calls to the SFA established that, if the case merited it, a commemorative cap could be issued. All we needed to do was get a copy of his birth certificate and away we went. Basically, to get Eddie's birth certificate, I lied. I rang his missus, Maureen, and told her that the club needed it for a reason and off I went to sunny Conisbrough, home of the castle, Ivanhoe and our former captain, to pick it up and see the man himself.

You are always welcome at Eddie's and it was even more important as he had just had a hip replacement a few weeks before and we do like to keep an eye on our boys when we can. As usual, he was on great form. A shirt had always been promised to Legends of the Lane, and this day would, it turned out, be the day that it was handed over.

Now, here is the thing. Eddie is a man of principle and he has always told me that, when his football career was over, that was that.

No dwelling on the past, no relying on former glories - you just moved on. Returning back from five successful years in the United States had seen him go into business and just crack on with life. Even as a player, the bright lights and pubs of Sheffield were never really his thing – a wife and two daughters to provide for meant that, after training or a game, home he went. It was as simple as that.

As a Blade he always had businesses away from football, a player that never earned more than £100 per week from the game saw that you had to speculate in order to accumulate and he did just that. A Blade who ran the transport side of a local business offered to put him through his HGV licence, so United captain and Scotland international Eddie did just that, ending up running several lorries. One Saturday a driver failed to turn in and a load of lime needed delivering to Lincoln. Not wanting to let the customer down he decided that he had enough time to do the job and still get to the Lane in good time for the game. The plan was going really well until the tractor unit broke down en route.

Add this to the fact that the club didn't know about this business and he had a problem. Thankfully the recovery crew got it running and he made it through to the ground - the only thing here was that it was in the lorry and he parked up on John Street with the full trailer set up and legged it into the dressing rooms to get changed with just 15 minutes to spare. No one even noticed! Eddie also took the licence needed to drive coaches and buses. Imagine the look of surprise on the faces of 48 pensioners on a Sunday day trip to Skegness on Sunday 22nd April 1973 when the driver looking after the coach was the Blades skipper, who had led the team to victory over Coventry City the previous day in the top flight of the English game. Truly incredible isn't it?

The presentation of Eddie Colquhoun's Scottish cap

This was also a player who had left school in his hometown of Prestonpans on the Friday and then got a train down to Bury on the Sunday to join the Shakers as a professional footballer. His Dad, who worked down the pit up there as a blasting engineer, had journeyed down to have talks initially with Bob Stokoe about his son signing for the Lancashire club and when Stokoe told him that his lad would be paid £15 per week, he literally fell off the chair. Long and dangerous hours down the pit paid him roughly half that amount, and that makes an interesting point.

Despite the colossal wages top flight players command today, Eddie always maintains that his era were far better off than the average working man and commanded a better lifestyle. No bitterness, no regrets. A young Eddie also played in the game against Sunderland that saw the prolific goalscoring professional career of one Brian Howard Clough prematurely ended, at just 18.

I may have said this before, but it is always a tale worth telling again. The shirts and reminders of a career that, for the Blades alone, yielded 430 full appearances had not been seen until my particular visit for over 30 years. They had been put away in a bag in the attic along with everything else and, in fact, the only indication of the years of playing was a picture of a little on-pitch altercation with Billy Bonds of West Ham.

One of the only players to be awarded an FA Cup winners medal and not play in the final doesn't even know where the gong is kept. It isn't an issue. It doesn't matter, and that's a fact. The Scotland cap was a long time coming and richly deserved. Ever reserved in his manner, he couldn't bring himself to say anything as it was handed over to him on the night by Stuart McCall, and I can promise you that he knew nothing about it. His family were there to be a part of it - they were so proud, and rightly so. He was a great footballer and is an even better man when you get to know him.

We are working now on a revisited former players' association, something which we value greatly at Bramall Lane. The 125 celebrations showed us all what treasures we have, how much they mean to us and you to them. We are a family, and that was one hell of a family birthday to attend.

CHAPTER EIGHT

BALL TO END ALL BALLS

FIRST PUBLISHED: OCTOBER 11, 2014
SHEFFIELD UNITED 2 LEYTON ORIENT 2
AND DECEMBER 31 2016
SHEFFIELD UNITED 1 NORTHAMPTON TOWN 0

How much would you pay for a football? The ones as a kid were always the seaside sizzlers – a couple of quid at best from the corner shop. One good kick and away they went; either over the fence into a neighbour's garden or up on top of the customary flat roof. We bought one on holiday in Cornwall this year to play beach volleyball. My youngest pointed out that, with me playing, it looked more like beached whale volleyball – he wasn't laughing when he got the sizzler bang in the kisser, though. Neither was I when I ended up chasing the paper light sphere down the beach with the wind right behind it every two minutes! But for a couple of quid it kept us entertained for a few minutes.

I also know, from experience, how dear a half decent example can be, and the way in which you have to guard them with your life from my time being around kids football. I have worked every one of the England U21 and other internationals in my time on the staff at Sheffield United and the balls they bring are counted out and then counted back in again with military precision. It is easy to see why... it's an expensive part of the beautiful game.

One of the true phenomena of the modern game is the signed ball. In fact, at one point it became something of a currency. There wasn't a charity raffle that took place that didn't have a ball up for grabs. The oldest one that I have ever seen came from the mid 1950s and had some great autographs on.

Hagan, Brook, Ringstead, Shaw – all barely legible after clearly being added to a leather case ball with good old fashioned Quink, but a real find for any Blades collector. It was given away as part of a Gloops club competition in the Sheffield Star and is a coveted possession in the family today. Apart from the sizzler, the first ball I can recall having was a Winfield case ball, bought from Woolies in Skeg Vegas. If you did cop one in the face it tended to sting a bit but you would get over it quickly. The Winfield though was a different prospect. Get that in the face or the wedding tackle and you knew about it. My Dad certainly did. First shot with that laid him out quicker than a sniper. I am sure that Dads weren't supposed to use that sort of language to their six-year-old sons, even after such an assault. It was with the first kick and probably the most unintentionally accurate shot I ever made, to be honest. I wasn't ever the most cultured of players. Wasn't even really a player, but there you go.

That Winfield ball that took Dad out also became my first ever signed ball. School holidays generally meant an excursion to the Ball Inn on the number 27 bus, a fair few of us would make that journey and a sign of the times is that there would be loads up there watching the Blades lads train. Cec Coldwell always made a point of coming over and speaking to us and the players also did the same when they had done. Now, this ball had survived years, by this point. They were truly indestructible and it had been everywhere with me. This particular day at the Ball was no exception - I had half a chance of being able to get out on the same pitch as my heroes for a kickaround before being chased off by the groundsman!

Anyway, this day the unthinkable happened. As ever, a few of the players came across to us to have a chat and, as usual, I was tongue-tied by Tony Kenworthy and Colin Morris. A few of my mates had a programme or two which they asked the lads to sign. TK grabbed the ball from under my arm and autographed it. "Bloody hell lad, we will have a whip round and get you a new one," he said. "Is this the best you can do?"

Scarred for life, and now with a football that clearly would never be played with again. That caused a few heated argu-

The 1915 FA Cup final ball...

ments when the time for a knockaround came around. No chance are we kicking this now, I said. I have still got it somewhere, and there's more signatures on it, pretty well all of the team that managed to get relegated to Division Four to be honest. I rubbed Don Given's moniker off it, by the way!

Down the years they have increased in number to a point that is beyond a joke. Not too long ago a nice one would get you £150 or thereabouts when raising funds, I have been present when they have struggled to make the cost of the ball and the time and effort taken to do them. That is down to the numbers out there, just check eBay out if you don't believe me – you can get a nice example from most clubs and eras for very little dosh!

We have the ball from the game at Hillsborough where Laurent D'Jaffo and Carl Asaba scored and the Leppings Lane end went mental. It was booted into the crowd by Laurent at the end and smuggled out of the ground by a few Blades. No mean achievement, and also a little naughty if we are being honest. Bless 'em! They handed it in here and I had to make a phone call to Wednesday's then-secretary Graham Mackerell. I think he thought I was taking the proverbial when I offered it back to him... clearly he wasn't too fussed about having the ball back from a game won by the Blades in their own back yard.

I have the ball from the Liverpool game, the first season back in the top flight, and the Redtooth collection in the museum has the very ball that Brian Deane changed the history of football with when he scored in front of the Kop with against Manchester United to register the first ever Premier League goal. However, a few weeks ago a kind fan donated something a little smaller but just as special to the Museum.

A member of their family had Darlow's Sports Shop on West Street and, back in the day, he used to lovingly hand craft small but perfectly formed leather case

...and the one from the 1899 final

balls to sell in the shop, and they are something special – a work of art. Now, as a Blade he took it upon himself to go and get a few signatures on it and chose quite a time in our history - the season when we lifted the Second Division championship in 1952-53. Alll the forwards got double figures and we had a tidy side under Reg Freeman, pipping Huddersfield Town by two points. The lads who made history are on the ball for all to see.

Ted Burgin in goal, Graham Shaw, Bill Toner, Len Browning, Harold Brook, Sir Jimmy Hagan; all signed the ball and, incredibly as signatures tend to fade through time, all are nearly as crisp and recognisable the thick end of 70 years on. You see plenty of autograph books, but this is just a little more special. All of those years on it still looks great and we were delighted to have it given to us. I don't know what it's worth and, in a sense, it is irrelevant. Someone kept it all of those years because it meant something to them, a bit like my Winfield case ball. I bet the lad who got it signed could remember every sweep of the pen by some great Blades names that helped write our history. I also bet they never played football with it during the school holidays!

What does a really rare example cost then? In my opinion, priceless. We have a couple of the rarest examples of them all at Bramall Lane, and they come in the shape of FA Cup final balls

- from that far off time when the ball you began the game with was the one that you finished it with. The 1899 ball came into my hands in about three pieces and a carrier bag over a decade ago following a tip from a fellow Blade, it had been in the hands of the same family in Woodseats for over 100 years and looked every bit of its age. Back in the 1960s a family member had borrowed it to take down to Bramall Lane for a picture on the hallowed turf. They took it with the warning ringing in their ears that it had to be looked after with their lives.

On arrival they ran into coach and former player Harry Latham, who decided that it would be a massive help if he undid the lace, popped a new bladder in, and simply blew it up. I mean, a fully inflated ball would look so much better on the pictures, right? Well, I am no expert on items lovingly crafted from antique leather, but I would like to think that even I would have known that dry brittle materials don't take particularly well to being blown right up for no good reason. This was no exception and this famous piece of football history literally exploded into several pieces. In a carrier bag it laid until I got my hands on it. We had to have the ball treated at the National Leather Conservation Centre in Northampton as it was actually disintegrating at a rate of knots; apparently suffering from a disease called 'red rot'.

The ball is 95 per cent there but has shrunk over the years. [Haven't we all?] It looks a tad battered but it is the ball that is in the famous picture taken at the side of the cricket pavilion with the FA Cup in 1899, and that makes it priceless – it would also be worth a small fortune if we were to sell it, but that will clearly never happen. The 1902 FA Cup final ball was kicked to bits on concrete, the son of winning goalscorer Billy Barnes told me that, as it was his Dad who kicked it to bits showing him the finer points of the beautiful game. It didn't work… he became an accountant!

The other one we have is from 1915, the actual ball from one of the most evocative games ever played in the English game and one of the few that is known by a name and not a year. The Khaki Cup final will be 100 years ago next April and remains the only final ever played during a World War. The Blades beat Chelsea 3-0 on a foggy, rainy, dank and dreary alternative to the usual fine weather and smiles associated with the showpiece game.

The ball had its silver plaque added after the game, as did its 1899 cousin. I mean, it would make a hell of a mess of your forehead when you tried to give it a nod, wouldn't it? The 1915 also spent most of its life in the same house in Woodseats, gifted to the family by influential football director and local fishmonger, Tom Bott. It is in remarkable condition, although it went down a different side of the family and didn't get subjected to the attention of Harry Latham at any point.

It surfaced in Doncaster and we were approached to bring it back to the Lane, which, of course, we jumped at. Both of the FA Cup final balls are worth a few quid, as you may have guessed. In Blades terms they are priceless, but in the world of football collectors they are highly sought after. The 1915 version would attract the interest of Chelsea, as it was their first ever major final; Manchester United would be keen as it is the only actual final played at Old Trafford, not a replay. And of course, it was our third win. The 1899 one is one of the oldest of its kind in existence, a real treasure from the Blades' golden era. Both can be seen on display at the club in Legends of the Lane. There would possibly have been three of them had a Victorian version of the seaside sizzler not taken place with the 1902!

High and laundry

I spent some of my happiest childhood years a stone's throw away from Bramall Lane in Heeley. Coming from Hackenthorpe was a bit of a shock at the time; Mum and Dad had newsagents on Birley Moor Road and a catalogue of bad decisions, at a time when times were hard, had seen them have to move on and start again. The other problem was that we lived in a flat above and, of course, that also meant we had to find a new home.

We had the usual things that you take for granted at the shop; a bathroom, inside toilet, central heating, just the basics you would think. But when we landed on Little London Place, it was like stepping back to the days of 'Fatty' Foulkes. For starters, the road was a cobbled street and still had gas lamps at the top and bottom. The toilet was outside at the top of the yard and the pee bucket became a feature of life for the next couple of years.

For reasons dictated to by a brother 18 years older than me, whose life revolved around work, his dog, football, speedway and the pub, I had to share with Mum and Dad. That can scar a young lad, I can tell you. It also meant not being able to switch the light on to have a wee in the middle of the night, and that could have fairly catastrophic consequences. Several times, after getting up and trying to locate the trough, I missed the footing and showered both my leg and the floor! There was one gas fire downstairs and, in the winter, it was freezing upstairs. The glass on the inside froze solid like a fly's skating rink and, as it warmed in the morning, the sheets became damp, and that was nothing to do with me or my leg!

The house had a cellar, as many did back then, piled with lots of stuff that had come from Hackenthorpe as there was nowhere else for it to go. I could weep when I think of what the damp destroyed down there: pre-war football programmes, Dad's cricket scorecards and a whole pile of other stuff that was just reduced to mush. It also used to flood as well. Not good when the Hoover twin tub was located down there for washing clothes. Even the fridge was at the cellar head and held in place by two spare car jacks!

The problem with the washer meant that it was easier to bag it all up, tie all to the remnants of a shopping trolley and take them down the road to the launderette on London Road near the White Lion. That was a place where some very strange people seemed to congregate, by the way; clearly the Garretts fitted in very well. The laundry department at the football club really is one of the unsung heroes of life in the game. Just think how many kits have to be washed on a Monday morning or a Wednesday after a night game - it really is loads, plus training kit as well. When I first joined the staff there was a top old lad by the name of Norman Goodchild, who did a lot of stuff for the lads up at the training ground and also ran the 'Dad's Army'

– the retired lads who cleaned the stadium after a game.

'Storming Norm' was well in his eighties back then and had spent virtually all of his life doing something for Sheffield United. His stories were legendary, and he could remember when the laundry for the kit used to be done by a lady on Lancing Road just off Shoreham Street. As a young 'un he used to have to collect all the shirts, shorts and socks and then take them on his delivery bike. They took it very seriously as well; one of his numerous journeys saw a couple of pairs of socks go astray and he had the cost of them stopped out of what little wages he got by then-club secretary John Nicholson!

Another character sadly gone is Peggy Platt. Peggy was taken on by Reg Freeman in the 1950s and was in the laundry right up to it getting a bit too much for her in the late 1990s. Back then, the laundry was in the old John Street stand and, after washing the kits, it wasn't unusual to see those famous red and white stripes waving in the wind out on the west terrace of the old John Street stand. That was back in the days when Sheffield's air probably wasn't the cleanest… in fact the smoke that used to bellow out of the Blue Anchor brewery across Cherry Street used to place a fair fog of pollution over our famous home. The smog was always worse in the hot weather as well - just right for spoiling the wash.

When she couldn't do the washing anymore Derek Dooley gave her the job of club tea lady. She knew how to butter a sarnie, did Peggy! Peggy was also landlady to a few of the younger players when they first came to Sheffield to try their luck as a Blade. Mark Todd and Martin Pike were two of her lodgers up at Low Edges and she proper looked after them. They thought the world of her and she gave them a real home from home back then - massively important when it comes to settling someone down in a strange place.

The laundry moved up to Shirecliffe when we moved up there and Mary and Sue were a huge loss to the ground. The laundry in the South Stand was a well-known point of congregation for managers, players, staff and directors - if you wanted to find out what was going on at the club or in the world in general that was the destination. Again, Mary was another character who carried on doing the tea and toast when she had retired – again, sadly no longer with us.

With kit manager Carl Hopwood still working all hours God sends, the operation up there is something. Sue is still sorting it all after well over 20 years, and it is a military style operation to say the least. What a lot of fans seldom realise is that, let's say we had played down at Plymouth Argyle and travelled back on the night, Carl would have to unload the kit skips off the coach into the van, transfer them up to the training ground and then sort everything out ready for the girls to wash and place in the correct player kit box the following day. No easy job… imagine what time he would get done!

These days the equipment is a lot better and so is the way that it is transferred around from A to B – no butcher's bike around to Lancing Road anymore, no drying shirts on the stand. The laundry is still one of the best places to find out what's going inside the Lane though!

CHAPTER NINE

THE CUP OF KINDNESS

ORIGINALLY PUBLISHED: NOVEMBER 28, 2014
SHEFFIELD UNITED 1 NOTTS COUNTY 1

Things in life always change, don't they? Think of the ground and how it was when you first came to watch the red and white wizards – how did it look back then? Chances are that if you are of a certain age then it bears absolutely no resemblance whatsoever. The changes in the stadium in the last 25 years or so alone have been startling to say the very least. That really kicked in with the Kop; go a little further back and the South Stand was opened a staggering 40 years ago next August – after a mammoth two-year build. Legend has it that it took so long due to a timber shortage. Even more incredible when you consider that it is built from concrete, but that is another story...

Bramall Lane opened in 1966 and was updated considerably in 2006. The pillars were taken out and the Westfield corner added – the view up there is both steep and impressive. Then there is John Street; up to the early 1990s that had changed little, bar what the Luftwaffe tried to do in 1940. The original stand was one of the most impressive ever built at the time and the very first commissioned outside of Scotland from Archibald Leitch, the Godfather and pioneer of the modern football stadia as we know it today.

Examples of his best work across the country are now very often grade two listed structures and they positively reek of what the game used to be about. Think of Fulham and you think of Craven Cottage and the Cottage itself. Now used for the families of players, it's a great example of what Leitch did... idiosyncratic, different. I saw the other week that Everton are well on the way to proposing a moving from Goodison Park, to me one of the great English grounds, and I really wonder what will happen to their Bullens Road stand – its trademark criss-cross iron work marking it as the work of the master.

John Street was a bold and financially incredible move at the time, and no expense was spared. It had a snooker room; players of the 1950s told me that the table was covered after a game and sandwiches and tea placed on the top. The only thing missing was their wives as they were not allowed in the stand – men only in such places. They would wait in all weathers in the doorway of the ice cream factory across the road for the lads to leave. Incredible when you think about it.

Other mod cons were on offer. It was one of the first in football to have a telephone line! Back then, game changing. Many will have seen the old pictures, pre-bombing, and seen the famous gable in the roof, again showing the famous Leitch ironwork as his signature. This was where the press would sit, compiling their reports on Needham, Foulkes, Utley, Gillespie and many more before the night the bombs rained down and changed many things forever. Again, this had many technical marvels of the day, but none more interesting than the carrier pigeon loft that was behind. The match reports would be com-piled, tied to the leg of one of the birds, and dispatched off to the relevant red top. A cheap and novel way of it getting there, I am sure you will agree.

There were other aspects that we take for granted today that were very game-changing in every sense of the phrase. The pouring rights of the club today command big fees, bonuses for the amount sold, and there are always many vying for the trade. Back in the day local landlords would submit the tender for running the bars at the ground. Our records show that, for quite a while, the landlord of the Big Gun in the Wicker was a firm favourite of the directors to quench the thirst of Blades fans on the day of a game. Beers doubtless served in a glass and not a plastic cup. Those really were the days, weren't they?

Non-alcoholic bevvies were the same, yet different. The warming drink that is synonymous with the beautiful game is OXO, and we were at the cutting edge where that was concerned. It was even advertised in the 1915 FA Cup final programme and in many a matchday read. The beef drink was available to the general public, but not in a paper cup – 1901 style it was served in a china mug, decorated in red with its famous name and logo for all to see. Your drink

The OXO cup which survived...

was served and then, when refreshed, they were collected in, washed and used again.

In the aftermath of the Taylor report and Bradford, the old order was finally changing and grounds were becoming a safe and modern place to watch the game. John Street had more wood than Arnold Laver and it was only a matter of time before the wrecking ball came a calling. I recall Reg Brealey signing the forms on the pitch before the last game of the season proclaiming a brand new stand on that side (it would be three years before it was finished and opened) and the demolition squad went to work.

I remember feeling sad as a big part of my life went to the floor over a period of weeks. That was the building in which the FA Cup had been presented by Sir Charles Clegg when Barnsley lifted the trophy by beating West Brom. Eddie Colquhoun had stood, fag in one hand, bottle of champagne in the other, celebrating promotion in 1971. Up to 1982, the players had always run out of that side of the stadium. It was where the dug outs were. It was Bramall Lane.

Much of the stand just went. The famous turnstiles were

saved; they were re-used in the new stand and gave many more years of service until the fully automated units were installed. They were then sold off to Blades and I am sure they make fantastic talking points in gardens and bars around God's Own County! Seats were thrown; wooden seats that had held the backsides of Blades legends were smashed. It was a sad time, but other clubs were doing likewise. It was change, progress.

Of all the things that survived the demolition, when all the rubble was being cleared, one thing turned up, one thing survived the destruction – one thing probably summed up football of the past, how it used to be and how it would never be again. In the rubble was a little chipped Oxo mug – a remnant of a different era. How did it survive? Who knows? It should have been smashed but it wasn't. A builder picked it up and years later, gave it back to me. It deserved to live and it deserved to come home to Bramall Lane. It had survived bombs, it had survived demolition, it had earned the right, and it sits alongside cup winners medals, caps and shirts – a reminder of what we used to be, and a worthy artefact to sit alongside anything else in the collection. And it's red and white!

CHAPTER TEN

CHARITABLE FRIENDLIES

ORIGINALLY PUBLISHED: SEPTEMBER 13, 2014
SHEFFIELD UNITED 1 ROCHDALE 1

The testimonial really has become a rare breed these days, hasn't it? The reason behind this is simple, in my opinion. The way football is these days, very few players stay at a club long enough to get one. Back in the day a benefit game, as they were known, was usually bestowed on a player as an inducement at the time of signing, and back in the day there were a few pearlers. 21st October 1901 – Celtic (no strangers to games against us back then) were the visitors for 'Fatty' Foulkes. The game was a 2-2 draw and 4,747 loyal souls turned out to show their support.

On 3rd May the same season, there was a Sheffield derby to raise funds for the first Ibrox Disaster Fund. Our captain, 'Nudger' Needham, had played in the England against Scotland game up there when the stand collapsed. Again, around 4,500 surrounded that worthy cause. These were different to many of the normal benefits of the day. It was customary to offer the part proceeds of a league game as a benefit to a player as long as it excluded the real 'big hitters' – Wednesday, Sunderland etc, where the revenue was a major boost to the club.

In fact, Sheffield United played an unwitting part in this rule being scrapped. When we signed George Utley from Barnsley, the reported fee of £2,000 was a record – a colossal amount of dough back then. Utley was viewed as the player who was the missing piece in the jigsaw, a leader both on and off the pitch to spur the club on to repeat its earlier domination of the game. The fee raised some eyebrows, but in his contract he was also offered the lease of the sports shop on Bramall Lane that had originally been under the stewardship of United coach George Waller. Many reading this would remember it in its last guise as Jack Archer's – a Sheffield institution for a good many years.

This was not unusual. A job or business was often used as an inducement, an income over and above what the club back then could legally pay the player for their work. The clause that raised eyebrows was the award of a benefit many years less than the normal. When the chance for this arose Utley took and was allowed one of the biggest league gates of the season – against the Mackems. The fact that the club allowed it caused a fair bit of unrest. It meant that he would stand to get twice as much as longer serving names including Billy Gillespie. Key players signed a letter of protest to both club and the Football League and even though he got his pay day, the league abandoned such rewards as a result. Bramall Lane had once again played a part in changing football history!

A benefit or testimonial could bring in huge crowds. Tony Currie's testimonial in 1986, a whole 10 years after he had last kicked a ball in anger for his beloved Blades, brought 17,500 worshipers through the gates of the Lane, the biggest home crowd that season! Famous names aplenty have turned up to show their appreciation to a colleague from the game. Jimmy Hagan had his showpiece match to mark the end of an amazing Blades career in March 1958 when a Sheffield XI played an International XI in front of an eye-watering 29,166 – a certain Brian Clough turned out for the visitors and typically scored. Joe Shaw was another. Our all-time greatest appearance maker got an All Stars XI to visit the Lane –29,500 were here to pay tribute to the great man, and here I get a great Hagan story.

Jimmy didn't suffer fools gladly and was forthright in opinion. When he arrived he was down to play for the All Stars. Jimmy called one of the organisers over and politely explained that, when he played at Bramall Lane he played in red and white stripes with the number 10 on the back. And whoever else they had in mind for that position could move on!

Jimmy, of course, got his wish. A nervous Mick Jones had the number nine peg next to the Lane legend, and sat down and introduced himself. Hagan shook his hand and explained to him that, at nearly 50 years old he did not intend to run around. When he asked for the ball he wanted it played to feet, not yards either side. If the ball was delivered correctly he would put young Jones in a goalscoring position and it was up to him to use it well.

Mick told me that he put the first pass a yard wide and Jimmy left him in no doubt as to the level of his displeasure. United lost 6-5 to the guests, although Jones and Hagan netted one apiece. Hagan went off after around 70 minutes to a standing ovation; the legend leaving the arena for one last time. When Mick got back in the dressing room there was Jimmy, washed, groomed and dressed immaculately in his England tie and blazer. Jimmy asked Mick his name again and then pointed out that, in his expert opinion, Jones had a few rough edges but he had seen enough to convince him that, if he carried on working hard, he could have a decent career in the game. Mick was gutted. At that point he had made over 100 first team appearances and been capped for England!

Testimonials have also been used to raise money in times of loss. One that sticks in my mind was for a goalkeeper called Keith Solomon. We had signed him from Truro City in 1980 and, by all accounts, he showed a fair bit of promise. He made one "first team" appearance in a friendly against Leeds United on 23rd January 1981. Just less than one month later Keith collapsed and died at the Ball Inn training ground during a session, and the club was stunned. At approximately 12noon, he had apparently gone up for the ball and literally gone down like a stone. Then player-manager Martin Peters tried to assist in reviving him, but to no avail.

United played his former club on 22nd March. I seem to remember that in fact it was played the following day as heavy rain got the match postponed and a strong side won down there 9-1 with an attendance of around 1,000. We played a pre season game against Truro many years later in 2001 for the "Keith Solomon Memorial Trophy" in one of Neil Warnock's early pre-season jaunts down there – it was good to know that they still remembered Keith, and nice that Sheffield United could be a part of it

More recent years have seen many others, but not for a while now. The last ones I can remember here and being involved in was Simon Tracey's, but, of course, and around the same time, Dane Whitehouse called time on his playing career following a horrific challenge at Port Vale. Who will be next? Who will be here the magic 10 years to get his chance? Chris Morgan must be in with a shout, and not many could be more deserving – I am sure not many would argue with that.

CHAPTER ELEVEN

PUBLIC CHANGES

FIRST PUBLISHED: MARCH 24, 2015
SHEFFIELD UNITED 4 SCUNTHORPE UNITED 0

Matchday routines seldom change, do they? I have been a member of the staff for more years than I care to remember, but the mates that I went to the match with when I was a free man still do the same things: meet at the same pub (if they haven't been closed and turned into a convenience store), have a beer or three and miss the kick off as a result. Creatures of habit, but that is the nature of the game. So much has changed around the ground in the last 40 years it's untrue. You only have to find a black and white aerial shot of Bramall Lane and the surrounding area to see that and you really begin to struggle. Sheffield is an ever changing place.

Let's go back to the pubs. Think of some of the ones near to the ground that you recall from childhood that were famous watering holes for generations of Blades wanting to quench their thirst. One I always remember was 'The Ship' on John Street, going towards London Road. Its real name was the 'Great Britain Hotel', named after the ship of the same name. You don't get pubs like that anymore and, if you did, they would be wrapped in cotton wool and preserved forever. It was literally like going into someone's house for a drink, or at least that is what it felt like as a kid with my big brother. It was like a bar in someone's front room - in fact, you could see the living room clearly behind the bar with the tea laid out on the table and kettle boiling merrily away on the stove.

It was an old lad who had it, proper waistcoat and fob watch stuff, sleeves rolled up and those armbands that stopped your cuffs from trailing in your soup. The smell of stale beer and tobacco smoke that is now a smell long gone from bars across the country, it got yanked down when the council started to finish the work that the Luftwaffe began in the late 1970s. I think the landlady was called Mary, I also think that they used to sell eggs on the bar that came from the chickens out back – a handy tool for anyone on the West Terrace!

Another brother hang out pre-match was the Bricklayers Arms on Hereford Street, near the corner of St. Mary's Lane. Again, all of that was swallowed up when they put the dual car-riageway through St. Mary's Gate. Famously, the huge church-yard that stood in front of the Church had to go as a result of the road and underpass. Both t'Ship and t'Bricky were beer houses, licensed solely for the sale of ales. No wines and no spir-its to be seen at all. That's something that you never see these days, either – the last one I recall is the Excelsior on Attercliffe Common. Again, long gone.

Many former players held pubs around and near the ground that are now also gone. One of the biggest losses of the last few years was the Sportsman on Denby Street. One of the very best pre match pubs that just went.

Graham Shaw had the place for a good few years with his missus, the lovely Beryl. Graham was some player and repre-sented the Blades and England with distinction; he also had a brilliant chippy in the markets as well.

I can remember looking at his England caps that used to sit in a cabinet on the wall above where the pool table used to be, towards the right as you walked through the doors. I used to find an excuse in my days working for an insurance company many years ago to skive off and have a couple of pints in there of a Friday afternoon with the man himself. A proper hero and a top, top bloke; sadly no longer with us.

As a fan who loves the history of the club, those are priceless memories. Not many players made their debuts at the age of 17 in front of over 60,000 at Hillsborough did they? The factories went and the students moved in.

They just didn't spend their money in the Sportsman and a piece of our folklore now lies empty and unloved. Tommy and

Connie Hoyland had the Sheldon a bit further up - again, that was a pub that I loved.

You got the best of both worlds in there – the big, bright back room or the traditional tap room at the front that hadn't changed in nearly 100 years. Again, it was always a warm welcome from one of our finest servants of the time, a Blade man and boy, who is one of those rare ones who also had a son in the shape of Jamie wear the red and white stripes as well.

Graham Shaw became a landlord

The building, as with the Sportsman, is still there. Sadly, not a pub. It is offices and student accommodation above. Another that has now gone and quite recently is the Vine on Cemetery Road, a bit off radar to be a real matchday watering hole in fairness, but still another loss.

That was where 1936 FA Cup finalist Harold Barton was host for some years, long before I came along. A bit further down was the Lansdowne, and I have been told this tale by several people. Always a busy pub, officials entered on the day of a game and calmly told staff to pick up any valuables and exit the building. Surveys conducted that week had shown the building was severely unsafe, possibly as a result of the extensive bombing in the area during the war. The only thing keeping the lot up was the keystone over the front door. When they removed it, the pub basically fell inwards! That's the story anyway!

Thankfully the Cricketers still survives, as does the Railway, Sheaf, Lion and Standard. It seems two minutes since you went to the loo outside in an open roofed affair just like the toilets used to be behind the Kop. Progression.

The Crown still looks good, starting place of the supporters' club in 1928 and just revamped along with the Albion, both under the watchful eye of Andy Rushworth. Two pieces of London Road culture preserved, thank goodness.

I have stood in the middle of the pitch many times 10 minutes before kick off in some huge games and wondered where all of the fans are. When I was writing this piece it became fairly obvious! Times change, buildings come and go, but we still have some fine pubs around our famous home.

We also now have our International Bar looking over the pitch where you can meet and talk the game before the first whistle. When they are gone they are gone forever, as the Sportsman, Sheldon, Bricklayers, Ship and many I haven't mentioned prove. All we have is memories of what went before. Progress sometimes isn't always for the better and the matchday routine and culture is a poorer place for it.

CHAPTER TWELVE

EVERYONE LIKES A BARGAIN

ORIGINALLY PUBLISHED: NOVEMBER 7, 2015
SHEFFIELD UNITED 3 WORCESTER CITY 0

A couple of weeks ago we had the Bassett's Boys reunion at Bramall Lane, reliving the successful 1989-90 campaign with the great man himself and his team. A great night was had by all and I'll write more about that in the next programme. There were some gems in that squad, a few bargains as well and it was on my way home from that night that my mind began to wander about cheap purchases that the club became renowned for way back in the day. Off the field, we have picked up a bargain or two as well as on it. Here's an amusing tale from a few years back which occurred whilst on club business.

I once went down to ELR Auctions when they were in the Nicholls building for a few bits and bats that I had picked up for Legends of the Lane. Back then our head of accounts was Dominic Field, a willing partner in the hunt for a fair bit of memorabilia with me. They had held a house clearance sale that same day. Dom asked if everything had gone, and it turned out that one unsold lot was a Hyundai Pony Car. Now, apparently in certain circumstances any unsold lot had to go, and if you made a bid post auction, then it could be considered as there was no reserve in place.

"Offer her a fiver," he said as the girl in the cash office peered through the window… and I did. She was gone a minute or so, then returned with the good news that we were the proud owners of a car for a fiver! I wasn't expecting a pristine car and I didn't get one, but it did have tax and test and a massive bonus was the fact that when I turned the key it started! The idea was this. Get it home, clean it, sell it, buy more footy stuff and Bob was your uncle. Just St Phillips and St Mary's Gate to negotiate. The £5 car crept out of ELR with me behind the wheel. I should add that I have always had 'any vehicle' insurance so all we were fine, dandy and road legal.

I crawled up the hill behind Dom, up to the roundabout. What a bargain! Heaters worked, radio cassette worked and although the window dropped into the body of the car when I attempted to wind it down, I was still pretty pleased with my 'bargain'. A gap came in the traffic on the roundabout and Dom was away. I didn't want to lose him as an alarming number of warning lights on the dashboard had now all begun to prove that they worked as well, so off in hot pursuit I went. The acceleration was fine, but the brakes were not. I did stop – that was largely thanks to Dom's Toyota Corolla as I ploughed into the back of it!

The Hyundai was remarkably unscathed. The back of the Toyota didn't look as good. Still, some new brake pads, a wash and hoover and we got £150 quid for the car on eBay, it went a little towards the £650 damage to the Toyota! A better bargain came in a box of old Sheffield Star and Green 'Uns from said auction. Half way down the dusty pile was a nice 1936 FA Cup Final programme that someone had just chucked in and forgotten about, worth more than 10 full boxes all together. That's sometimes how it goes.

What about football players? What is the best bargain that you have ever seen arrive at Bramall Lane? There are sadly less and less that saw Jimmy Hagan join from Derby for a bargain £2,925 reported fee. Mind you, I bet that would have bought you a fair bit before the war. Maybe a few more around saw Alex Forbes arrive with his boots in a brown paper bag, for a fee of £40 which increased after appearances to a hefty £105!

Doc Pace wasn't a bad shout from Villa for £12,000 as a late Christmas present in 1957, and he weighed in with 175 goals in 301 games. Doc always seems to me to be one of the great United players that tends to get overlooked in terms of his contribution. Tony Currie caused John Harris to persuade the Board of Directors to stump up £26,500 for an 18 year old. Ted Hemsley always points out that he cost £1,000 more than TC, so that must mean he was a better player!

£160,000 for Alex Sabella? Big gamble back in 1978 for a largely unknown prospect, but what a player for a young fan to hang their hat! I thought the world would change when the Argentine came in. It did. We got relegated! I am sure that others will have different views on their best bargain, but for me in the midst of many, there is one deal that for me and in my time really stands out above the rest.

Dave Bassett had an eye for a player, of that you can never argue. Look at Brian Deane, Tony Agana, Alan Kelly… the list really is a long one. For me it was Simon Tracey, in a deal from Wimbledon. Shortly after, another player that I loved for what he did for United made the same journey, in John Gannon. 'Trace' came as cover for Graham Benstead initially in October 1988 and went onto gain two promotions and make 380 appearances for the Blades over a 14-year stint.

He could have played for the Republic of Ireland in the Jack Charlton era and was robbed of the chance of joining the England squad to train due to a shoulder injury. He was a true club player who always gave everything to the cause and cracked on even when he lost his place on occasions. Gannon also served the Blades well. You look how much he was involved on the park in terms of assists, tackles and passing; he played in over 200 league and cup games for United and I always felt that, at that time, we played better with him on the pitch. The crowd could get at 'Ganns', but he never let us down when the bullets were flying. A proper Blades attitude.

Between them they cost just over £12,000. They also made over 600 appearances and played a huge part of the rebuilding of a tattered reputation of a club that had gone through the mill. They helped us get back to the top flight, play Premier League football and reach heights that a generation thought had long gone. Oh, and both were far better looking and worked a lot better than that Hyundai Pony!

CHAPTER THIRTEEN

STANDING FOR FORTY

ORIGINALLY PUBLISHED: AUGUST 15, 2015
SHEFFIELD UNITED 2 CHESTERFIELD 0

Forty years ago, Bramall Lane was a very different place. Since football took hold, the famous ground had been three-sided – cricket had sat side by side with football and the famous pavilion had looked out over both at that point for over 70 years. There had been a couple of attempts to finally sever connections with the summer game once and for all since the 1960s and various options had been discussed over that time.

The club had even carried out a fairly in depth feasibility looking into relocating the whole show to land at Jordanthorpe with a 40,000 all-seater stadium. Thankfully it was ruled out and we stayed at 'home'.

The baby finally kicked out its mother when the club decided that, to progress forward and be a major force once again in the game, cricket had to go. A new South Stand would rise over the wicket, making Bramall Lane a true four-sided stadium for the first time in its long and proud history.

Started in 1973, the stand took nearly two years to be completed and made its full debut on 16th August 16th 1975 – 40 years ago tomorrow – in the old First Division when the opponents were Derby County.

A crowd of 31,316 were here to witness the future as the South Stand opened its turnstiles for the very first time. Commercial activity and football really began to run at this point and a full on diary of entertainment went into full force on that sunny afternoon. It really surprises me 40 years on as I walk around the pitch just how little room there is at the edges.

Yet on that day all those years ago, cars from Heeley Bridge garage - that included MG Roadsters and Austin Princesses - were driven right around the perimeter.

Even more alarming were the lorries. Laver have always been massive supporters of the football club and they turned up for the celebrations. Huge lorries followed the cars around, loaded with piles of timber (and scantily clad and very un-PC potential Miss Sheffield United FCs) giving out goodies that included 'United Kick Off with Arnold Laver' stickers – the pictures we have show the huge beasts in front of the then new stand in an area in which you would struggle to get a wheelbarrow down today.

MC for the day was local DJ and Hallam big cheese Keith 'Cardboard Shoes' Skues, resplendent in his obligatory very white and extremely flared suit. One of the original 'Pirates of the Airwaves', he led the advent of commercial radio in the Steel City.

He, I believe, is still plying his trade somewhere in deepest darkest Norfolk although there is no truth whatsoever in rumours linking him with a certain Alan Partridge. Back of the net indeed!

An Austin Princess, for some reason, pulled a caravan round (probably because Bessacarr Caravans of Rawmarsh were also sponsoring) behind it – that was a result because every time I saw one of them it tended to be being towed behind a truck or pushed by someone who strangely looked like Keith Skues! There was then the majorettes and dancing girls and on the back of the shirts was Arnold Laver branding for the world to see. All exciting stuff!

All this warm up began at 2pm – former players from both sides of the city that included Redfern Froggatt, Graham Shaw and Albert Broadbent took part in the 'Arnold Laver Supershot Competition' and Broadbent scored with all six to be presented with a silver salver by Alan Laver and Derek Dooley in front of the Kop.

I can well imagine the warm and friendly reception the former Wednesday favourite got from the red and white faithful to commemorate his win at the home of football.... I was there

and funnily all I can recall is boos and abuse.

The season before had seen the Rams win the Championship again under the management of Dave Mackay. We had finished sixth and been in the frame ourselves right up to the wire, still our best post-war League finish in the top flight. The game against Derby was a 1-1 draw.

We opened up with a penalty from Keith Eddy - what a player he was on his day by the way - and Charlie George, one of the original mavericks, equalised in the 82nd minute.

A season that set out with so much to look forward to went disastrously wrong. We were, in effect, down by Christmas. Manager Ken Furphy parted company with the club, Jimmy Sirrel came in and so did the rot that saw us end up in Division Four.

Many companies still around today had worked on the project. Electrical contractors Lillekers, who hold our contract today, had done the installation for both stand and floodlights. The work had mostly been done by Sheffield companies; it had been designed in the first place by Husband and Co. and the main contractors had been George Longden and Co.

A workforce of 150 had welded 650 tons of steel and moulded 5,000 tons of concrete into the shape that we still see and

use today and the work hadn't been quick as we have seen.

It's hard to imagine that the areas that now take up the museum, Platinum Suite, ticket office, superstore and reception as well as offices, boardroom, dressing rooms and many other utilities were, up until the early 1980s, just empty voids. You could actually park cars there.

The cricket pavilion stood and watched the change and progress that would eventually see it razed to an undignified pile of rubble at a later date. A chairman who never seems to get the credit he deserves for his early tenure and the developments, by the name of Reg Brealey, masterminded that change and made Sheffield United a business with the very best corporate facilities in the city at that time.

Had the council rubber stamped his plans for the Bramall Lane centre around the same time, they would have had nearly all needed to avoid the cost years later of the World Student Games. But that is a very different story.

So happy birthday to the Laver Stand, Global Windows, Top Spring and whatever else the South Stand has been known by since that day 40 years ago.

As you read this, just imagine the changes that it has seen; the great players that have run from the tunnel, the tens of thousands of meals served, pints pulled, pies warmed, tears cried, songs sung. The hopes, the fears and the highs and lows. The stand and its cost at the time could have finished United, but the brave move to build the striking modern 1970s structure changed the destiny of the Blades and the face of its famous home forever, for better and for worse. It's part of the Lane and therefore part of us.

CHAPTER FOURTEEN

OLD PARTS

ORIGINALLY PUBLISHED: MARCH 1 2016
SHEFFIELD UNITED 2 BURTON ALBION 0

What's the oldest part of Bramall Lane? It could well be Mick Rooker, couldn't it? He seems to have been around forever. He actually lives at Bramall Lane, you know. In a hole under the Kop. Well, it seems like that. You can come down to the office at any time and find his car in the car park. He will normally be messing around with Super Draw memberships or wrapping presents for one of his 985 Godchildren. You'd be forgiven for thinking it was Mick, but you would be wrong.

Most of the stands are built within the last 50 or so years. That said, the Kop is the oldest in continuous use. After the Taylor report, we made it all-seater and put a new roof on, but the basic structure has been in use since around 1902. Back in the day local industry was encouraged to dump waste over a period of time which was compacted into a 'mound' onto which the terraces were added. It's not unusual to turn up Victorian clay pipes and bottles when you do any work on there, it was an open stand until club director Richard Lawrence put the cover on in 1936. What a man he was. The owner of 'Laurel Blades' – the city's premier razor blade manufacturer and great philanthropist, he also built the open-air swimming pool at Hathersage. During the

Mick Rooker

Blitz, concerned for the safety of his workers, he drove from a village on the outskirts of Sheffield, to his premises on Nursery Street, to check that all was well. His staff were sheltering in the cellar of the place with the bombs raining down. He went to them and, shortly after, the building sustained a direct hit - resulting in many deaths, one of which was the great man himself. Ironically, the roof he had funded a few short years before was also blown to pieces during the attacks.

Back to the matter at hand. Is it the cricket pavilion clock that's oldest at the Lane? Well, that's now above the entrance to our museum, Legends of the Lane, and has seen many happenings at S2. The clock dates from the second pavilion, or the one before the one that some of you may still remember with a great amount of fondness. Its famous face has looked out over historic events aplenty. Ashes Test cricket, the FA Cup final, the club's early faltering steps, England games, and semi-finals. If only it could talk, what a story it would tell. But it isn't our famous clock.

Inside the museum are stained glass windows. They date from the very first cricket pavilion and are famous the world over. They have been photographed for more books on Sheffield sport than Tony Currie and, in two beautiful pieces of glass, tell the story of Bramall Lane. Football and cricket being the two biggest parts of the tapestry of our famous home. They have been in position all over the ground over the years; in the John Street stand, boardroom, sponsors' lounge. They are much loved and have done well to survive the ravages of time and the wrecking ball that has decimated much of Sheffield over the years. Close, but there are still older bits if you know where to look.

One of them will be the wall that runs the length of the Bramall Lane edge of the ground, or at least the footings of it that you cannot see from the road. That is made of big sandstone blocks and is quite possibly the remnants of another Bramall Lane first that helped shape the world of sport. The walls that defined the Lane as being more than just a field or expanse of land that people just used for sport were completed in 1865, along with the very first refreshment booths. These were located towards the John Street side of the stadium and were also an important advancement in sporting facilities.

The wall meant that the land was very much separate from that around it. Don't forget that, at that point, there was another bona fide football ground just at the other side of Cherry Street in the shape of the Sheaf House Ground. Many of our neighbours staged games there back in the day and, although smaller than our home, it was still very much there and open for business. The booths were put out to tender to be run by local publicans and we have records that show that, a little later on, it was the host of the Big Gun pub on the Wicker who had the monopoly over that for a fair number of years; long before the battle for pouring rights became a major issue on the commercial calendar. The Victorians must have had a good way of building such things, because the current structure has been supported well for many years - since 1966 to be accurate - and all was well enough to modernise the stand over a decade ago. Clever lads those Victorians. The truth is that many of you will have seen what is possibly the oldest part, or at least structure within the stadium footprint and walked past it on many occasions. It would be fair to say that a good number of us started our love affair with the Blades from the Kop end, so we are back there on the oldest stand again.

There have been several structures on the Shoreham Street side. A Championship flag flew proudly from the roof of the stand at the beginning of the 1898-99 season - the wind all but blew the thing down - but it is really nothing to do with that. If you have ever entered the ground from the highest turnstiles on John Street to start the long ascent up the stairs to the back of that stand, you will have walked past the banking that is covered in trees and foliage that now forms the back of the corner stand there. That in itself has been there for years, a real remnant of when the stand was born many years ago.

That is underpinned by an old stone wall, it's been there that long that it just fades into the background. That fact, coupled with it actually doing a pretty good job of holding the banking

back and stopping the whole lot from sliding down, has probably saved it from the ravages of time. In that corner, when the bomb damage of the Blitz was finally rectified in the early 1950s, was once a very functional concrete staircase which disappeared when it was finally pulled down in the early 1990s. The wall there arguably comes from the days long before Sheffield United were even thought of and goes back to a time when a very different ground echoed to the sound of willow on leather in the summer, one where the highlight of the year was the annual sports day.

It will have stood silently whilst Sheffield FC took on Hallam FC on 29th December 1862 in the first ever football match at the Lane, when Thomas Youdan instigated the first ever cup final in football, when Fatty Foulkes stalked the penalty area and Arthur Wharton changed the world. It saw Barnsley lift the FA Cup, the Aussies take on the English in the Ashes, soldiers recruited to fight in the war. It is a time machine that has stood silently watching the world change and it has done it without comment. It is a part of the original boundary that set all of this history in motion and it has done its job well and without complaint.

I wonder if the builder who put it there all of those years ago ever thought that it would still be there and doing its job? I wonder if he thought that the ground was a good idea or if he ever thought that the rough game of association football would ever take over from the gentlemen's world of cricket?! It was there before the football and has seen a hell of a lot of change.

CHAPTER FIFTEEN

TUNNY DUNNIT

ORIGINALLY PUBLISHED: DECEMBER 28, 2015
SHEFFIELD UNITED 3 BRADFORD CITY 1
AND FEBRUARY 4, 2017
SHEFFIELD UNITED 4 AFC WIMBLEDON 0

It's great to see a club of Leicester City's size having a crack at the Premier League. Now, to be honest, I seldom watch any football other than my beloved Blades. It doesn't really bother me and I don't really ever connect with it. I would far sooner go and watch Sheffield club or Hallam in non-league if we have a blank in terms of fixtures. I also get far more of a kick watching my junior club sides on a Sunday. England games have also become much the same. I think it is a connection thing. If I'm not involved to some extent, I'm not overly interested.

Some of my best memories as a kid came from the Saturdays that, for whatever reason, Dad or big brother couldn't take me to wherever the Blades were playing, which meant a short walk with the old man to watch Frecheville. Still a cracking little ground in the middle of suburban Sheffield to this day, I loved going in the old wooden clubhouse that had been built by a mate of Dad's – the smell of hot sausage rolls and Bovril served in real mugs was something special, along with the community spirit of all up there.

If the football wasn't that great, there was a lot of fun to be had doing forward rolls down the banking or getting up to no good behind the little Kop stand that is still very much there today. There was little wonder that the ground on Silkstone Road was also a regular venue for the local semis and finals.

Dad was a very good referee. He went into it a little late in life as he played until a decent age and also followed United.

It was a reaction of desperation when the Blades appointed Jimmy Sirrel and the great slide began; he just got fed up for a while. Keith, my brother, managed the Manchester Hotel in the Nomads League, they were decent as well. In a semi involving them and Deerstalker, the opposition went up and scored a goal that to all bar the ref - which happened to be Dad - was a yard or more offside. Big brother went berserk and his use of the English language was a little colourful, to say the least.

Dad warned him that, if he carried on, he would be watching from the car park. The same fate awaited him also if he carried on referring to him as 'Dad'.

"It was offside," he protested.

"No it wasn't," countered Dad the ref.

"It was," he continued.

"Want me to prove it to you?" offered Dad.

"I wish you would," was the last line of defence.

"Buy the Green 'Un on Saturday and read the score."

He had a point, I suppose, and a fairly good one. He was right; the goal definitely stood in the Green 'Un the following week as did the fact that they didn't win the game as a result of said allegedly offside goal. Meals were interesting at home for a while. Anyway, back to the Foxes. Jamie Vardy has been banging them in and took the Premier League goalscoring record - good on him. Even though he supports the dark side of the city, he was released by them as a young 'un and has done it the hard way via Stocksbridge Park Steels, Halifax and Fleetwood and others and has, as a result of his hard work and endeavours, also got international recognition. It's a fine advert for kids never to give up and keep trying.

However, it is a Blade in Jimmy Dunne who still holds the top flight record for scoring in consecutive games and until the recent wave of publicity, his goalscoring talents were getting overlooked. Dunne was an Irishman, born in Dublin, who had played Gaelic Football at first.

As a young man he found himself in an internment camp for his sympathies to the Republican cause before being recommended by a scout at Brother Christie's club, Shamrock, to then-

Jimmy Dunne

Football League side New Brighton. The Blades spotted his potential and secured his services in February 1926, for a reported £800 fee.

There was no magical debut straight into the first team. Harry Johnson still ruled the roost and Jimmy had to wait for his chance. When he got it, he exploded. His first hat-trick came, ironically, against Leicester City on 7th September 1929 and that was followed by successive four-goal hauls against West Ham and Leicester again. Jimmy would be our top scorer for four consecutive seasons and set the Vardy-chasing record by scoring in 12 consecutive games - beginning against Grimsby Town on 24th October 1931 and ending on New Year's Day, 1932. All in the top flight of the English game.

As a Blade he also bagged 15 hat-tricks (12 in league games) and his total of 41 goals in the 1930-31 season, plus five in the FA Cup, is still a club record. He also netted four goals in a game on four occasions and got five in a friendly. Truly incredible stats. The local papers and the Green 'Un coined the phrase 'Tunny Dunnit', as he formed a formidable understanding with FA Cup legend Fred Tunstall, who supplied many of the pinpoint accurate crosses from which he benefitted greatly, as history shows. Billy Gillespie and George Green had him very much under their wings, so 'Snowy' - as he was known due to his white-blonde hair - was in great company to say the very least.

He left us for Arsenal where he played a part in the Championship-winning side of 1934 before representing Southampton and then returning to Ireland. This remarkable man also played for both the FAI XI and the IFA XI as an international, winning 22 caps. In 1935 we attempted to bring him back to the Lane to play with Jock Dodds, imagine how frightening that would have been. Sadly cartilage issues stopped this, or the numbers for the club could have been even more impressive. He finished up as player-manager with spells at Bohemians and Shamrock, but died tragically young of a heart attack in November 1949. His gravestone, we are told, has a picture of him in his United kit. The Blades were clearly never that far from his affections.

Jimmy's grave

The Blades connections do not, however, end there. One of his sons played for Jimmy Hagan at Peterborough United and also represented Leicester City. His other son, Tommy, sadly passed away earlier this year. He was a legend at St Patrick's Athletic and many will know their strong connections with members of the Handsworth Supporters' club branch that have blossomed over the years. They have an area in the ground commemorating the late and much missed Chris Booth and their lads come over here to support the Blades regularly over the season. Records were made to be broken and Jamie was close but no cigar. When you get a minute, check out Jimmy's records – they are truly impressive.

As the records will show, Vardy didn't manage to break Jimmy's record, but I am sure that the Premiership winners medal, media attention and England caps that have followed helped to sweeten things a little. What his attempt did do, however, was encourage the younger members of the Dunne family to finally get in touch with us to connect with something that they realised was very special to Jimmy – the Blades.

His gravestone did indeed carry a picture of him in his Blades kit. We also found that the grave and picture was also not in the best of shape as the ravages of weather and time had taken their toll. The picture, set in a small glass frame, had suffered from the damp badly; giving us a chance to do something fitting. Working with the family, we were happy and honoured to contribute to having all made good and to replace the original picture like for like.

It was an honour to have played a small part in remembering one of our former sons who has lain there for so many years - it kind of felt as though we were remembering his achievements and making sure that anyone walking past his last resting place saw that he wanted to be remembered as a Blade first and foremost. We were happy to make that happen. Jamie may not have taken the record away from Jimmy, but what he did do was link the Blades and the Dunnes back up again after all of those years. Another member of the football family came back to the fold.

He's not bad for a Wednesdayite that Jamie Vardy, I suppose.

CHAPTER SIXTEEN

BAND ON THE RUN

ORIGINALLY PUBLISHED: SEPTEMBER 12, 2015
SHEFFIELD UNITED 1 BURY 3

Bruce Springsteen played Bramall Lane twice. That's fairly well documented and a bit of a Lane landmark. Not my scene to be fair - all that American Dream stuff didn't really sit well with a lad off the Scowerdons, to be honest. But there is no doubt about the standing he has in modern pop culture is there? You could hear it for miles around as well. I remember having a beer outside the Birley on the Saturday night and, as the wind changed direction (very Clash) you could get a snippet of his set. Tunnel of Love tour, I think it was.

Although it was our first concert proper by a significant artist, football grounds had been doing it for years. The Who actually played a series of gigs at football stadia in the mid 1970s - the Vetch Field, Celtic Park, and a gig recorded as one of the loudest ever at Charlton Athletic. As usual, United were at the very forefront of the idea back then, long before the Electric Light Orchestra played St Andrews or Wembley played host to Live Aid or big Bruce came to town.

Who did the Blades target? What was the plan, I hear you ask… There were some behemoths of bands in the early-to-mid 1970s to choose from. The Rolling Stones were huge draws on the back of such landmark recordings as Sticky Fingers and Exile on Main Street. Led Zeppelin had served up 1V, Houses of the Holy and Physical Graffiti, making them arguably the biggest grossing act of their time. The Eagles had flown over the Atlantic. David Bowie could have been a strong contender and even our own Mr. Joe Cocker would have been a pull on home turf, not long after being one of the Mad Dogs and Englishmen.

Bruce Springsteen, in concert at Bramall Lane

With all that great talent we went for one even bigger… the pull of the moment… bigger than the Bay City Rollers… trendier than T Rex… more special than Slade.

We talked with the biggest boy band of them all, the Salt Lake City 1D, the one and only… Osmonds! Donny, Jay, Merryl, Jimmy, Dave, Dee, Dozy Mick and Tich (a few are correct). The South Yorkshire music scene trembled at the very thought. Forget Brown Sugar, Trampled Underfoot or Hotel California. Who needs FM music staples and legendary rock when you can have Love Me for a Reason and Crazy Horses? The Bramall Lane machine swung into action to tempt the clean-living Mormon boys to our world-famous home.

A professional early version of a PowerPoint was commissioned to put to their advisers, who were listed as 'Loco Promotions of Leeds'. Guess what? Yes, I have a copy in my archive. Let's look at what we had to tempt our very own teen idols with in the middle of the decade that taste forgot, and talk you through the pitch…

The Stadium

A lovely shot looking from the south side of the ground across the Bramall Lane stand at the lovingly once red and now peeling pink eaves of the John Street stand with St Mary's gazing over on a fairly grey and typical Sheffield day. This is followed by a shot of the Lane end from the Kop – the Sheaf Motors advert and supporters' club clock look resplendent. A shot of John Street tells us that 'the vast majority of spectators are under cover at the stadium'. 'Backstage' there are many facilities including superbly equipped dressing rooms (we had a bath and a couple of ashtrays), catering and the directors' private suites (that would be the snooker room!).

Others show the South Stand nearing completion with the assurance that, even in its unfinished state, it could be utilised solely for a stage and be secure from all remaining sides of the ground! It was clearly decided next to sell the merits of our beautiful and very green city. I never hide my love of the place of my birth and its many merits, but let's see what we were using to snare our quarry, and I don't mean round Little Jimmy's neck, although after Long Haired Lover From Liverpool...

'Ideally Situated'

No arguments there. Bang in the centre of the country, new million-pound stand nearing completion and built for large crowds. It mentions that the biggest was 68,287, but not that it was in 1936! Aah well, only 40 years. The authors then took us on a closer look at Sheffield, with panoramic shots of: Town from Norfolk Park, the Town Hall and Peace Gardens, the Hole in the Road by Christmas lights, the University and a picturesque view in the snow of the Gleadless Valley estate, long before This is England saw the possibilities of filming there. Finally in this section we sold the idea of our luxury hotel industry back then. The Hallam Towers was the big daddy and they tell us that, at the height of their popularity, the Beatles stayed in one of them and no-one ever located them.

The final part relied heavily on the now famous "Sheffield – City on the Move" campaign that former Blades press officer Pete Wigley played such a big part in and, years later, announced the arrival of The Full Monty. An impressive argument for Donny and the flared five, and no mistake. A letter now tucked inside the presentation tells the story of the outcome...

"As a result of negotiations with Loco Promotions of Leeds and the Graham Poulter Organisation, fruitful discussions took place with the Osmond's agent. Due to adverse publicity received concerning Bramall Lane ground safety in the Sunday Times on Sunday, March 16th 1975 [must have been the gents at the back of the old Kop] negotiations were broken off and no further progress has been made on this subject. It was proposed that a two-day pop concert was to be held at Bramall Lane and the consequential loss in revenue to the club was estimated to be in excess of £60,000. This does not take into account television facilities, fees, commercial ventures and catering concessions."

Negotiations were also in hand for the Evel Knievel Show. Now that I would have liked to have seen but again, due to the unsatisfactory state of the ground from a spectator point of view, that was a no-go too - with an estimated £8,000 profit for the club going up in smoke! So, we missed out on the Osmonds and Evel Knievel but we did get The Boss in 1988 - with around 88,000 people, it was reported, heading to S2 for the two shows.

Unfortunately we don't have documentation of the sales pitch to get Springsteen to Bramall Lane, but we hope that the powers that be learned from the lessons above and simply sent him a greasy chip butty, pint of magnet and a packet of woodbines, and that they sealed the deal!

CHAPTER SEVENTEEN

ERNEST AND HIS RULES!

ORIGINALLY PUBLISHED: SEPTEMBER 15, 2015
SHEFFIELD UNITED 2 COLCHESTER UNITED 3

Life is all about rules, isn't it? From the moment we are old enough to know what is going on, we are told what we should be doing and how we should be doing it. That goes from your parents and family first and then into school. When that part of the system has chewed you up and spat you out, then the big boys get a grip and then there is no way out! Stand up, sit down, walk, don't run, no mobile phones, no vaping, no parking, no diving… the list goes on.

Football clubs have rules, all are the same and for reasons. As an ex-smoker I get the 'no smoking' rules in the stands. No standing, well, that one will always be a contentious subject in the game. Racism and its consequences goes without saying, I have never considered the club that I love to have had real issues here. That doesn't mean that I haven't encountered the occasional idiot, we all have, but the main thing here is that it is never tolerated, never stomached - and quite rightly.

Players, of course, have rules. Both as a professional representing their club and as a figure out on the pitch. That is what the referee and his assistants are there for. Life is full of referees but on the day of a game they have to control all of them along with the 18,000 or so managers that will be present. The captain plays his part too; helps keep control of the situation, calm the flashpoints, enforce the rules. We have had many great skippers down the years, all different, all adding something to the role. Morgs, Pagey, Reg Holdsworth, Stan, Eddie, Cec… the list is endless, but history shows that one of the earliest was arguably one of the best.

Ernest Needham was born in Chesterfield on 21st January 1873. He joined the fledgling Blades in 1891 and would spend the rest of his life associated with Sheffield United FC, in one way or another. He would lead the club to a league championship and three FA Cup finals, winning two. Known as 'Nudger' and described as the 'Prince of Half Backs', he also remains our most capped England international and was one of the first professionals to skipper his country.

A total of 16 caps today seems a pittance, but back then the only games would have been against Scotland, Ireland and Wales. That means that when fit and available, he was a mainstay in the side for nearly a decade... well over 100 caps in today's money! He was the first player to write a book. 'Association Football by Ernest Needham' isn't exactly 50 Shades of Grey, but it broke the mould. He listed CB Fry and GO Smith, amateur sports pioneers as well as legendary batsman 'Ranji' – Needham was a county class cricketer as well, by the way! When he signed for United, he was given a rule book.

I know that because we still have it in the club's collection and it really does make fascinating reading. It has 'Mr. E. Needham' written across the top and I was flicking through it only the other day. It is visible proof on how the world has changed, let alone the game and its structure.

It was issued by JB Wostinholme, our secretary, and gave the office address as 10 Norfolk Row - as well as the president, ground committee and even medical officer, J. Stokes, practicing at 82 Ecclesall Road. Just to prove it was true and not concocted as a fable, the club colours are listed as 'blue knickers, white shirt with red stripe' – there you go! The bye laws are clear. All players (whether amateur or professional) shall appear in 'proper football costume' – later it also states that players will be provided with an outfit and they will be held responsible for any loss or damage sustained on their part.

Every player is also told that they shall keep it clean and in good repair at his own expense... no swapping or throwing to the crowd there then! The captain is instructed that he is responsible for returning the ball to the storekeeper immediately after the conclusion of the game and every player is reminded that they shall keep themselves in 'fit and proper condition' and turn up to play at the place notified. If unable to do so then a medical certificate was needed.

Sponsors and mascots back then would also have been in trouble... it specifies that only players and committee members are allowed in the dressing rooms and that the trainer, Jack Housley back then, will be in attendance on Tuesdays and Thursdays (midday and evenings) and at any other time required by the committee for training purposes.

'Nudger' as a Blade

Every player, wherever possible, is required to turn out on these days, placing his name in the training book as a record of attendance to be submitted to the secretary and committee on a weekly basis. Just like a school it seems! The team was announced by way of being posted in the dressing rooms on Thursdays and players residing in the town must 'accept this intimation', whatever that means!

The Blades back then were members of the Northern League. The first XI kicked off the 1891-92 season at home with a friendly against Middlesbrough Ironopolis on Tuesday 1st September, winning 5-1. Two days later saw Millwall Athletic despatched away 2-0 and we were off to a flyer. I know this because Ernie was good enough to lovingly write the scores in his handbook! Needham played 554 games for his club.

What must it have been like to have seen the transition from Northern League to major football power, to have bridged the gap between amateurism and professionalism and lift the first major silverware achieved by the club?

Scouting until his death in 1936, little more than a month before our last cup final appearance against Arsenal, I wonder what he would have made of the club he gave so much to today. The way that players, manager and supporters conduct themselves. The ground, the kit… the fact that the captain no longer has to take the ball back or take his own kit home and wash it?!

He would probably have felt more at home with the comeback of substantial facial hair though. Any picture of the great man displays a finely sculptured handlebar moustache… he would have got on great with John Brayford!

I suppose that the rules must have worked. Look how the game developed and how quickly it happened. Thankfully this one little book survived world wars and time itself. It sits there and reminds all of what used to be, a colour look into the black and white or, in this case, red and white, of what went before. Maybe rules aren't such a bad thing after all.

CHAPTER EIGHTEEN

A SHORTAGE OF SILVERWARE

ORIGINALLY PUBLISHED: OCTOBER 20, 2015
SHEFFIELD UNITED 3 FLEETWOOD TOWN 0

We haven't seen a lot in the way of success over recent years in terms of actual silverware, have we? I mean, the last time we actually lifted anything of note was before talking films and not long after the First World War. Form is temporary, class is permanent after all! Apart from 1961, when we should have beaten Leicester in a succession of replays, for years we never came near. Even the great John Harris side at the end of the 1960s was, frankly, awful most seasons in the cup competitions. The season we went up, Portsmouth dispatched us 2-0. Brian Clough's Derby saw to us in round four the previous year and Mansfield Town the year before. The magic of the FA Cup certainly hadn't sprinkled its dust on the Lane.

If you are a Blade of, say, 40 years old and you started watching us when you were seven, all you have seen, in our terms, is unbridled success. I never supported us because of potential European Cup finals or Premier League titles. Not much chance of that. Like most of us, I had no choice, that's who we supported and what we were, in it for the long haul.

Let's look at the facts, and the 1981-82 season as a start to the theory. A great side... Keith Edwards, Colin Morris, Tony Kenworthy, Darlington and the Fourth Division championship. Good start there and then 1983-84, promoted again under Ian Porterfield. Dave Bassett's first promotion came in 1988-89, followed the next year by yet another on the back of a couple of fairly credible cup runs. In 1992-93 we were founder members

of the Premier League and FA Cup semi-finalists at Wembley, our first visit to the national stadium in over 50 years.

Moving forward just a few years; 1997, the play-off final against Palace; 1998 FA Cup semi-final against Newcastle at Old Trafford; 2003 League Cup semi-final against Liverpool and FA Cup semi-final against Arsenal, plus the play-off final of the same year against Wolves at the Millennium Stadium. In 2006 we were back to the Premier League in some style; three years later we went to the play-off final at Wembley against Burnley. We were back there in 2012 for the play-off final against Huddersfield whilst very recently there's been the FA Cup semi-final against Hull City and last season's League Cup semi against Spurs.

Scary, really that, in those years as a fan, how many times we have played at Wembley? As a kid I would watch the FA Cup finals with the family and dream what it must feel like to be doing it with your own club and not trying to decide which team you would support on the day for the sake of argument. Which, incidentally, was usually anyone bar Leeds or Liverpool! A mate of mine, who is a lifelong Evertonian, gave me some sage advice when we got through in 1993. I recall him saying: "Wembley is great, enjoy the day and always remember the moment, but it's a long way back when you lose." He was right… as we Blades have found out on many an occasion.

That said, in our lifetimes, we have seen far bigger and potentially lucrative Blades games than several of the generations that have gone before. More cup semis, more Wembley trips, more genuinely big moments than our Dads and Grandads. I remember my brother getting on the coach he ran for that first trip to the Twin Towers since before the war and saying "Next stop Wembley, I have been waiting 43 years to say that" – it really summed it up better than I ever could have. Prior to all that heady success and barring the County Cup, there was one fleeting chance of a pot for the boardroom cabinet came in the form of the long lost pre-season tournament known as the Watney Cup – we lost to eventual winners

Derby in 1970 then took our chance again in 1972.

The competition was a knockout affair for the teams that scored the most goals in all four divisions that had not been promoted or qualified for Europe. The cup also saw the first English penalty shootout in the 1970 semi between Hull City and Manchester United. The first ever one was taken by George Best, the first miss was by Denis Law and that was saved by Tigers 'keeper Ian McKechnie. Incidentally, he then became the first player to miss a deciding spot-kick in that game. Who said pre-season games were boring?!

In 1972 we had seen off Notts County 3-0 with goals from Woody and TC (he got a brace) and the Posh by 4-0 (Mackenzie, Dearden, Hemsley and a Woodward pen) – that set up a final against Bristol Rovers at Eastville on a red hot 5th August. The game has been written about in these pages before - so has the fact that it was Ted Hemsley who missed the deciding penalty. The goal that could have written his and the Blades' name in Watney Cup history!

The lads all got a small silver tankard simply engraved "Watney's Invitation Cup Runner Up 1972" - someone must have been having a laugh as it is also marked "Rand English Pewter - Made In Sheffield." It would have been cheaper to have just picked it up round the corner from the Lane as opposed to travelling all that way to lose and cart one back again, wouldn't it? Ted's nearly didn't make it back at all. He was so narked at both losing and missing the decider that his got launched at the dressing room wall and then stamped on.

That game was also one of my very first away adventures as a nipper. All I remember about it is how hot it was, how big the gas tanks looked behind the ground and how fast the bloke carrying the matchball fell from the sky with his parachute delivering it. You can't do that anymore - the lad landed on the top of the stand before the first game of the season, after the wind changed.

The game was held up for an age until they got him off the roof at Ashton Gate! It set the standard for my luck with cups from that moment on. We have one at the club and it's another part of our history, for better or for worse. I keep it locked away with the Yorkshire and Humberside Cup and the Cisk Trophy we won over in Malta. One day, our day will come.

CHAPTER NINETEEN

SCARBOROUGH FAIR

ORIGINALLY PUBLISHED: MARCH 3, 2015
SHEFFIELD UNITED 1 PETERBOROUGH UNITED 2

There are times in life that, years later, you look back on with a real sense of pride - that you were there and a part of things. Family life throws loads up, like the birth of your kids (we lost 5-0 at Ewood Park the day my youngest was born on 1st April 2000). I was in and out of the delivery suite at the Northern General until an exasperated sister had a right old go at me. She just didn't get it; neither, to be honest, did his Mum. Nor clearly did our defence at that time! The eldest got away a little better, he was also born on a Sunday but we didn't have a game. No birth suite issues there, though he was nearly born in Pizza Hut on Wellington Street. Super Supreme would have been a great pair of middle names!

Working for the club has also given some wonderful memories. I looked after the mascots at Old Trafford when we played Arsenal in the FA Cup semi-final of 2003 and what a day that was. Amy Warnock had the job and her Dad got us into the United dressing room, usually a no-no at the Theatre of Dreams. As my opposite number stood and fumed in the tunnel for half an hour because he didn't have similar access, we sat and had a brew with the lads.

Manchester United didn't let people out on the famous playing surface, but we wangled out the old 'it is our cup final' routine. We were told to go no further than the edges, but once we had approached Amy's favourite player (Rob Kozluk) we - that is myself and photographer David Pye - were never going to turn back. There were at least 10 Paddy and Max lookalikes ready to pounce as we finally came off the pitch. That was capped with walking out of the tunnel with the team as the noise from the Stretford End threatened to take the roof off the stadium. I could have died happy that night; a real case of living the dream as a Blade. Monty turned to me as we walked to the dugouts and had tears in his eyes. Fantastic stuff and a time in our history that it was a privilege to be a part of.

Another such event happened recently and had nothing really, per se, to do with football, more to do with our historic home and its birthday. When United were 100 years old it was quite a party; we had a big reunion dinner and there were loads of events to mark the centenary.

The club also commissioned a painting as a sort of birthday card to itself. We did prints, albeit a limited number, and they were used for match sponsors with a few available as numbered items, signed by Dave Bassett and the squad. Lovely things and very collectable.

Now, the picture was the work of Joe Scarborough – one of the City's best sons. If you have ever had the pleasure of even the shortest amount of time in his company you will have had a warmth shine over you that is quite unlike anything else you will find. It brightens up even the darkest, dampest Sheffield days with the same colour that radiates from one of his creations.

His works rightly command huge fees and are much sought after - they really are special and it was for that reason, added to the fact that the centenary one is so much loved by all at the club, that he was asked to do the same again, but this time telling the story of the Lane and its life and times over 160 years.

Joe lives and works on his canal boat that is moored up at Sheaf Quays and I was invited down to see the work nearing completion. I had bits of input in terms of pictures, timeline and marking important events that could be brought to life, telling the story of our famous home.

Several things struck me. One is that there isn't a lot of head room on a barge, even for someone vertically challenged like me. I found this as I nutted the roof backing in as instructed. The second was how big the canvas was. It seemed to take up

Amy Warnock with
Michael Brown

the whole space - an incredible sight in an area so confined.

It was then the masterclass started. No room to move for four of us, just a seat close together and an insight into a real class act and the way his mind works. The loving explanation of each scene, each piece of the Lane's life added to the way in which the picture has grown from the first day that the paint was added.

Truly fascinating. I mean, how you put so much life into a piece, all the thousands of voices? The hopes, the fears, the happenings and history. The way his eye works is so different, and even the thought process of how the figures in the story and their journeys is there.

The trams, the houses, the reasons. Life.

It's not all about football, not even sport. Music is there with Bruce Springsteen, religion with Billy Graham, the skyline shows Abbeydale Picture Palace looking on as it has done since the 1920s and there are also the barracks on Edmund Road to the other side. Harry Houdini, master escapologist, practiced walking the high wire in there during an engagement at the Empire or Hippodrome and its ramparts are a familiar part of what has always surrounded the ground.

Cricket, World War One recruitment, Empire Day; all the past was there to see for the future – memories of what once was and what still is.

There can be few pieces of land in any major city that has helped play such an important part in the lives of the people that live there. Forget football loyalties... Bramall Lane is only partly about that when you begin to really look at what has happened on those acres of green land since Michael Ellison came up with the idea to have a place that was to be 'free from smoke'.

And what an idea that was. Joe has immortalised 160 years, in oil on canvas. We have had the honour of filming the great man actually explaining his work, his train of thought and ideas, the recipe for what is one of the most stunning works telling our story that has possibly ever been done.

CHAPTER TWENTY

KEEP IT IN THE FAMILY

ORIGINALLY PUBLISHED: NOVEMBER 14, 2015
SHEFFIELD UNITED 2 SOUTHEND UNITED 2

You can't beat a family get together. To be fair, there are that few of mine left you could hold a decent bash in a telephone box, but all the same, they are events to be savoured. Most of the ones I can remember as a kid tended to end with my Dad falling out with one of his brothers and not talking. The record was 20 years and it only ended because he dropped dead. Now that's being really stubborn, isn't it?

The idea of getting together and reminiscing about times gone is one that has always appealed. My eldest uncle was a good 10 years older than Dad and was one of the dark horses of the family - he was a Wednesday fan, albeit a seriously lapsed one. He lived in Grimsby and never had a car, so maybe he had an excuse.

He was there in 1935 when they beat West Brom to lift the cup for what is the last time. He was so chuffed that he prom- ised his Blades-obsessed younger brother, namely my Dad, that if United ever got there again, he would take him to the game.

Unluckily for him we did it the following year and met Arse- nal at Wembley in the showpiece final. He was as good as his word and took him to the game. Just to hear them talk about the games, the journey, the players back then… it was truly magical. Families are always on the move, they seldom stay in the same place and life gets very much in the way at times. They become spread as jobs change, houses are moved; it's like the tide, when you begin to think.

I have said before that Sheffield United is very much like a family - a big, extended one, but a family all the same. In the years that I have been here, there are colleagues that have become more like brothers and sisters - in fact I spend more time with them then I do my own. You share in the happiness, success, hopes and fears.

The ride is a rocky one at times, but it makes the good times even more enjoyable, even more memorable. Many go on to new jobs, new places to live and new opportunities. Some you will always keep in touch with, others drift. That is just how it is. On October 24th we celebrated 25 years since Bassett's Boys clinched promotion back to the promised land of the top flight - back-to-back promotions at that, a fact made even more incredible as the squad that he put together cost relatively little.

The team spirit of the lads was something to be marvelled at. It was one of those occasions when the recipe was just right, the mix of qualities and character worked and to spectacular effect. I think that is fairly well documented and the results really speak for themselves; history seldom, if ever, lies. They were great days to be a Blade. A quarter of a century… wow!

As I welcomed those coming back to the champagne reception in the club museum, it was just like welcoming family back home after being away for too long. Sheffield seems to hold former players of both clubs here - they like the place and the people so much that roots are put down and ties that will last a lifetime are well and truly made.

Simon Tracey is still here. So is John Gannon, Peter Duffield and Mark Todd, whilst Carl Bradshaw, Mitch Ward and Dane Whitehouse are born-and-bred. Tony Agana and Paul Stancliffe are in Rotherham, Brian Deane is in Leeds, so not that far away from the action. Dave Bassett remained here until a few years ago, Derek French is still in Sheffield, so that must say a lot. Chris Wilder is another born-and-bred Blade still here, even though he plies his trade in Northampton.

It may not have escaped your notice that the 'Cockney Mafia' was very much a big part of the thing back then but they are all adopted Sheffielders now. For the great night a couple of weeks ago, others went to greater lengths to be here.

Graham Benstead came from down south and brought his

lad with him. Paul Wood and Mark Morris travelled together from near Brighton to be part of the fun. Martin Pike lives in his native north east, but loves any excuse to return to the club he still loves - despite leaving it to become a bit of a legend at Fulham in one capacity or another.

The camaraderie is such that others who didn't even feature in that team and came later also wanted to be at the get to-gether. Glyn Hodges and Paul Beesley were along for the night, and quite right too. They played more than a part in a successful era.

Over 350 fans wanted to be a part, not just fans but family members. Blades family members who all just wanted to re-member the very best of times and pay tribute to a great man-ager and a top bunch of lads.

None of them cost the earth but all were prepared to sweat blood for the cause, never hide and always give 100 percent – exactly what this great club has always been about. Legends are built on the back of such endeavour and memories are etched indelibly in the minds of all that were a part of it, whether it was from the terraces or the offices or the dressing rooms.

It was a special team and a special time. Dave Bassett made it possible for fans that had been dragged through the mill by the scruff of their necks for too many years to really believe again, and the lads who were there on the night delivered that and many more dreams to hungry football souls.

Bob Booker couldn't be there, and was devastated. Work and family commitments down on the south coast just got in the way, but rest assured he will be back at his spiritual home sooner rather than later. Colin Hill was the same. Life just gets in the way at times but there will be other chances, you just have to make them.

Look at the pictures for the family album and enjoy them as much as the boys did that night. Good people, good company and a net full of fantastic memories. To me, none of them ever change. Heroes never do - they still look exactly the same as they did 25 years ago and still mean just as much. Thanks to all the lads for all for the memories of back then and the ones you create every time you come home. That's truly what a family reunion is about - and what a great family to be a part of Shef-field United is.

CHAPTER TWENTY ONE

HAGAN TALES

ORIGINALLY PUBLISHED: NOVEMBER 24, 2015
SHEFFIELD UNITED 2 SHREWSBURY TOWN 4

I will always argue that, when asked to put together your all-time best Blades side, you actually have to have seen all of the players you pick play. When we have done all-time XIs, I have seen some great names added in. Needham, Gillespie, Foulkes, Dodds, Johnson – the list goes on. All greats, all United legends and many responsible for major honours. Sadly, there are fewer and fewer around still fortunate enough to have seen any of the names listed play. Maybe the odd one saw Jock Dodds as a kid, but none who saw Needham and Co.

I mean, how do you pick a player on what is effectively hearsay? Thankfully plenty are around who saw Woody, TC and the like. Even the era before that, filled with Pace, Simpson and Coldwell. But the generation prior to that has less and less. Jimmy Hagan is a name that will always be mentioned. I never saw him anywhere near a football shirt, but the name is one that is always synonymous with quality – by all accounts, a player that all agreed was years ahead of his time. One that should have had a bag full of international caps, not just the one recognised post-war appearance against Denmark in 1948.

Signed by Teddy Davison in 1938 from Derby, he was the son of a former professional player. Jimmy had been a schoolboy international who had been signed by Liverpool as a 14 year old, but fell victim to a Football League ruling that he was, at that age, too young to join their ground staff. He returned home to Washington in the north east and eventually signed for Derby, making his debut in the Football League just before his 18th birthday.

According to sources and the history books, his United career is legendary, mostly played out at a time when there were very few cameras recording games, so there is very little visual evidence. A few fleeting Pathe seconds against Stoke, a bit for the Football League, but most of it is passed down through families. My Dad said Jimmy was the best he ever saw, with TC as a very close second, and I would never doubt the old fella when it came to the beautiful game.

Our neighbours from S6 clearly thought the same. In February 1951 they offered a then record fee of £32,500 for a player past 30. United's board, incredibly, accepted, but Jimmy didn't. Known as his own man in every way, he refused point blank, saying he would finish his playing career with the Blades. He was a football rebel, as well. Many well-known names from the English top flight allegedly travelled to Ireland to play for cash under assumed names, meeting at places like Fishguard to get the ferry together. Shamrock may well have benefitted from Jimmy's talents.

Not many people realise but when he had taken his United bow, he also played for Blackpool. OK, it was on a tour abroad, and done as a favour to his great friend Stanley Matthews, but a Tangerine he was for a short spell! Jimmy's first job as manager saw him take Peterborough United into the league for the first time in their history. Allegedly, they were joint top of the table with Northampton Town and the directors had decided that they were not entirely happy with the squad that, at that time, were looking strong contenders for promotion. So they urged Jimmy to spend money and strengthen.

Most would jump at the chance, but not Jimmy. He maintained that none of the players available for the price the Posh could afford were better than he already had and refused to spend the money just for the sake of it. That proved the last straw in a few stand-offs where the great man stood his ground, and they parted company. West Bromwich Albion were the next to spot his talents. His vision and training methods were far ahead of their time, one of the first real tracksuit managers, and this brought him into early conflict with players at The Hawthorns. In the winter of 1963 the temperature dropped well below freezing, and the players stepped out at the Baggies' Spring Road training ground wearing track-suit bottoms. Jimmy ordered them to take them off and they all refused point blank.

The players went on strike for several days. Jimmy could be a hard taskmaster who accepted only the highest standards. To prove a point, he carried on training sessions with the younger players, who had not joined the action, in shorts and with sleeves well and truly rolled up to the elbows. The media loved it and it made headlines for several days. Even medical experts got involved and confirmed that the risk of inju-ries was heightened when limbs were cold, but he still wouldn't back down.

Jimmy Hagan

A few weeks later, he accidentally reversed his car over the canal bank at their training ground. Eyewitnesses saw the vehicle somersault down the steep bank, landing upside down on the towpath before bouncing into the water and landing the right way up. Rumour is that several of the players debated whether to help, but all were amazed when they got to the scene to find him crawling through the broken windscreen onto the bonnet of the car before making a scramble to the bank. A hard man in many ways.

Jimmy led the Baggies to two League Cup finals and created a strong side, before the two parted company and he went onto a spell working with old friend Joe Mercer as a scout for West Ham before becoming one of the greatest managers in Benfica's history - coaching some of the greats, including Euse-bio, who rated him as the best he had ever worked for. Jimmy's principles brought the end there as well. Eusebio's testimonial game saw players of the calibre of Bobby Moore fly to Portugal to play, the Benfica committee told the manager what team to play - and he told them to mind their own business. When they wouldn't, he promptly resigned. Eusebio went round to the Hagan residence himself to beg a change of heart, one that didn't happen. He was never a man to go back on his word; not as a player, not as a manager, not as a man.

When looking for work in 1968 he was invited to a meeting with the United board at the Hallam Towers Hotel in Sheffield. John Harris was moving upstairs and the Lane legend was seen as the ideal man to lead the revolution. His questions were simple... were certain senior figures still involved? When the answer was 'yes' his reply was short. The chance to bring him home had passed. Despite this entire hard and cool image, this was the man who, from the sports shop he ran on London Road with friend and playing colleague, Harold Brook, would deliver an ordered gift to the house of the child receiving it on a Christmas Eve. He would also put a protective arm round many of the part-time players that would train with him on a Wednesday evening at the ground.

Above all he, and his family, were and are modest to the last. Son David, still very much a Blade, would play football with his pals at the top of Meersbrook Park, not far from the Hagan home. He never told any of them who his Dad was - which worked well until one day he turned up to fetch him. You can imagine the effect that had. Plenty of lads calling for him at home from that moment on!

There you go. I try and touch on life and times away from the Lane and still never really scratch the surface of the story of the great man, I can still think of more anecdotes and tales writing this. I was lucky to have met him on a fair few occasions, and you always knew you were in the presence of United greatness. Jimmy died in Sheffield and his funeral was held at St Mary's on Bramall Lane, in the shadow of his beloved Blades. Like I say, to put the greats of yesteryear, such as Jimmy, in your all time XI you have to have seen them play.

But my Dad said he was the best, and that's good enough for me.

CHAPTER TWENTY TWO

CARAVAN OF LOVE

ORIGINALLY PUBLISHED: JANUARY 23, 2016
SHEFFIELD UNITED 1 SWINDON TOWN 1

What an awful year 2015 was in terms of losing Blades-men. Shred, Alan Woodward, 1952 Championship winner Howard Johnson, Ken Furphy and Howard Kendall all passed to a higher league. Then, in December, we lost Alan Hodgkinson followed, the very next day, by Martyn Harrison, our long-serving photographer. At one point someone suggested that we should have a permanent black armband as a part of the kit design for next season – the usual football black humour, but a fair point. We spent so much time mourning loss last year that it was untrue.

Of course, I knew Shred. Who didn't? I had met both Howards and Ken before, but Woody, Hodgy and Baldy were good friends. I got to know our former players through working for the club and thought the world of them. Because Woody's visits were less frequent due to him living in the States, they also tended to be the most expensive as he did like a pint or four of proper beer when he was over here. I tended to get roped in with him as a willing accomplice. Bless you, Woody – my liver sends its fondest regards.

Hodgy was like your favourite Grandad . He was just a lovely, genuine, brutally honest legend who loved Sheffield United, without question. His regular phone calls were looked forward to, as were his and wife Brenda's regular visits 'home' for the game. She often said that she suspected he would sooner be at Bramall Lane than with her at home. Sometimes she may have had a point! I don't like funerals, but sadly, over the course of a year, I seemed to have a season ticket. My relationship with

Martyn was slightly different. He was not just a work colleague, but a very good mate. Because he was a Blade, I knew him before we worked together, but getting to know him, you quickly realised that he was a thoroughly nice bloke – not many had a bad word to say about our Baldy. He was good company and would do anything for anyone. As long as they were Blades, of course.

Cookie, our programme editor and part of our media team, had many adventures with Baldy. They travelled to away games together over many years, spending hours and hours sitting side-by-side talking absolute rubbish. Travelling together saved time and money and also swelled the coffers of the De Rodes Arms at Barlborough - the owners of that establishment should be able to retire on the profits of Cookie and Baldy's countless visits for all-you-can-eat breakfasts on a Saturday morning or a carvery ahead of an evening trip.

One of my favourite Baldy tales is from a weekend at Exeter we had a few years ago. It was the last game of the regular season and a few colleagues took the opportunity to have the

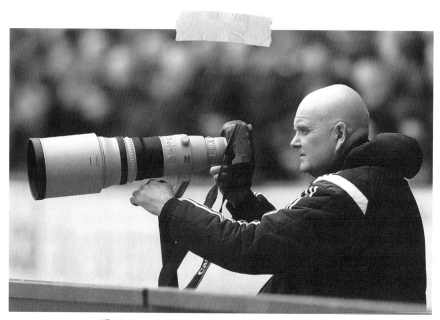

'Baldy' in his typical matchday pose

weekend away. As well as Baldy, Cookie and myself, there was Richard Batho, who worked with us a few years ago, and Dave McCarthy, our operations guy. The idea was a good one; travel down together in a mini bus, have a night out in Devon, go to the match the following day and then come back to Sheffield en masse. Simple and a real plan, especially as there was still all to play for in the game.

We organised transport and designated Richard as the driver, so all we needed were some digs for the night on the doorstep of St James Park. All good so far. Dave Mac did the research and announced that he had sorted a caravan on the biggest caravan park in Europe, located in Exmouth - a short drive away from our destination and all for the unbeatable price of a tenner a head, split between those going. What could possibly go wrong?

The journey down was a doddle, we arrived at the caravan site in good time. Too good as it happened, apparently the caravan wasn't ready, but the bar was open so we relocated for a couple of hours. A couple of us had Blades-related shirts on and we were accosted by a lad who was originally from Gleadless, had lived there a good many years and was a Blade as well. Thankfully he knew where the caravan number was (not far from him), which was a good job as we would never have found it in a million years. He also produced some tea bags, milk and sugar – top man.

Now, as I have said, this was the biggest caravan park you have ever seen; hundreds of the things. Pretty well every other rental van was fairly new and quite palatial. Ours looked like the one Mum and Dad had in the 1960s, I think it was a Bluebird. The worst on the whole park. The curtains had been thoughtfully closed to hide the true horrors awaiting the bargain holiday makers. It was truly gothic; bright orange stained velour upholstery, brown carpet, brown walls, brown cupboards and even brown water when you turned the brown taps on. The television worked at least - well, if you wanted to watch just ITV. We sat and looked at each other, stood and looked at each other. It was no use. We went to the pub.

JG (centre) with Kevin Cookson (left) and Pete Stone

Now, we turned up in Exmouth on the day that it was either shut or had been evacuated. Mind, we had sunk a few and had a good craic, but I was one of the first back to Chez Grim and that's when it dawned on me that the night was going to get worse, for two reasons. One, I was sharing with Cookie. Two… him and Baldy were a nightmare when drunk together.

They returned somewhat refreshed in the early hours and in good spirits. The caravan lurched as Cookie's ample frame slid into the bed at the side of mine. Baldy was next door. Now, at some point that week, some idiot had been daft enough to upload a version of the CD that Ronnie Sharp did, of all the old Blades terrace songs. Now, in the wee small hours, Baldy wanted to share the tunes with his travelling companions. "I love you JG," cooed a sloshed Baldy as Ronnie belted out a Lane classic… funny for the first hour. I politely advised where I was going to stick his iPhone if he didn't stop, whilst he nearly fell off the bed in the next room as Cookie turned over at the other side of a paper-thin wall.

The following early morning (I am always up first) I got my own back. Apparently, if you throw bits of remnant pizza on the roof of a caravan, the gulls attack it like a scene from Pearl Harbour, hitting the roof like hailstones and waking up drunken colleagues. It was funny. When Baldy finally raised his head, I think it was his idea to try and lure a gull into the caravan with bits of banana, strategically putting pieces towards the shower, where Cookie was trying to clear his head. I don't know who was more petrified when they came face to face, Cookie or the gull?! It wasn't a nice sight for the gull, that's for sure.

The game was much less fun, I have to admit, but Baldy was one of the very best and any time in his company was a pleasure. Many of you will know that anyway, but it was a fact. A top man, top Blade and a top snapper. Away trips will not be the same without him.

CHAPTER TWENTY THREE

QUICK CHANGE

ORIGINALLY PUBLISHED: APRIL 17, 2017
SHEFFIELD UNITED 3 BRADFORD CITY 0

Many Blades are former pupils at City School and I'm sure they will agree that it was a brave man who ventured down for a pee at break time back in the day. Designers in the 1960s seemingly decreed that the most accessible toilets would be down in the changing rooms, and these were located down in the bowels of the building near the sixth form block. There could be any one of several perils awaiting you on your journey in that direction to answer the call of nature, including the wall of death, which consisted of what seemed like around 500 lads from the years above lined up on each side of the corridor like an aggressive human wallpaper.

A second year (I think they call them year eights now), generally with an Adidas bag twice the size of their own body mass, would then have the tough decision as to whether or not they needed the loo badly enough to run the gauntlet. Oh, I still remember those screams. There are laws against this now, thank goodness; character building it wasn't, but you learned how to run fast, I can tell you! I suspect it was similar in most schools in the 80s and 90s, but I can speak from experience at City.

The changing rooms in any sport are the very hub of everything. Where plans are made, tactics discussed, banter instigated, the very heart of any sporting team. When Rob Kozluk was a player here at the Lane, there was an initiation ceremony for any new players coming in - each had to bring a gift or tribute to the changing room fraternity. It started off fairly small and then got well out of hand; there are statues up there, I think at one point there was a pinball machine and also a flashing leopard skin toilet seat that played the theme from 'Only Fools and Horses' when you lifted it up.

The changing rooms at Bramall Lane today are a far cry from the ones of old. Luxurious, clean and warm, each player has their own 'bay' in which their kit is all laid out and ready for when they arrive by Carl Hopwood, our long-serving kit manager. They have music (loud and generally awful) to up the pre-match tempo and also a TV to divert attention further, along with the usual showers, baths and modern amenities – very nice they are too.

A far cry from the days when local players used to get changed in recycled railway carriages like the ones that they used to have down at Drake House Lane when I was a kid, and the green huts that were dotted around many Sheffield parks before the trend of burning them to the ground really caught on. The smell of damp, stale urine and Ralgex was a part of any weekend football unless you were fortunate to be graced with the use of something as exotic as a working shower, like at Graves or Concord.

At Bramall Lane, we always seemingly had decent facilities; you can tell from the old ledgers that we were ordering coal to fire the boilers that made the water warm for the baths. Sheffield United was always created to be a major football club, playing at a major ground and challenging back then for the highest honours that could be gained. Many of our neighbours had more humble roots in a sense. Our neighbours over the city had played at a fair number of grounds before they landed at their first serious home, Olive Grove, a short cricket ball throw away from our famous base.

I once read a Green 'Un from around 1910 where they interviewed one of the original Wednesday committee from back in 1867, and he told a story of them playing in Norfolk Park and getting there bright and early to mark out the pitch and set up. It also said that, in the absence of any changing facilities for the players, they would pay local children hanging around to watch the game to look after their clothes after getting changed behind a convenient hedge. Very al fresco!

United's dressing room area in the 1950s...

If we agree that Bramall Lane is one of the oldest major professional grounds, in the city that gave the very foundation stones of association rules to the world, then all else emanates from around a quarter of a mile of our boundaries. Across Cherry Street was another bona fide football ground, The Sheaf House. Wednesday played their very first games at Cremorne Gardens, a Victorian leisure area that stood roughly to the left of where Rossi's restaurant has been for many years. Sheffield Club took their early steps on a pitch on Strawberry Hall Farm Lane; their centre circle would have been roughly in the middle of what is now the B&Q on Queens Road, and the rest of the first pitch swallowed up many years ago by the advancement of the railway line.

Hard to imagine that Olive Grove was a major ground before that too had part of its land swallowed up by the line to London. It had stands, terracing and I would love to tell you that it had the best of changing facilities for a team on the verge of major success, but it didn't. Now, if you are of a certain age and

...and a more modern day set-up at Bramall Lane

you enjoyed a few pre-match beers, there is every chance that even the most diehard Blade has unwittingly stood and had a few pints of Wards bang in the middle of Sheffield Wednesday's changing rooms of yesteryear because, back in the day, the others used the now gone Earl of Arundel and Surrey on Queen's Road.

In fact, it was their registered office for a time for admin and supporters. Imagine that - a derby game against the mighty Blades and Needham, Foulkes and Co. are getting ready for battle against the enemy of Crawshaw, Brittleton and the rest of them, in the back of a boozer two minutes away from their own place to walk across the road, over Havelock Bridge and in through the players' entrance! I mean, they could have just got changed at home and walked down, couldn't they? I have never ever seen any evidence to support either, but if that was the dressing rooms then surely that's what happened.

Bear in mind that this was top flight football, by the way. These days the team would probably get the coach to take them across the road! Hard to believe that major honours were won on this ground and when the lease of the land was ended by the then Duke of Norfolk to sell the land to the railway, the main stand was dismantled and taken over to the current site on horses and carts. There is a plaque marking the site, which is now the council works depot behind a bus stop on Charlotte Road.

The Earl was a lovely old pub, now sadly lost to time. It's a bicycle shop now, so at least the building was saved from the wrecking ball. Incidentally, it was the last Pound House in the City - that meant that whoever was the landlord had a legal requirement that, if someone found and brought a stray animal to them, they had to feed, water and house it for a period of 30 days. I wonder if anyone ever happened across a roaming swine of pigs and dropped them off for the landlord to sort?

I'm not going to say anymore!

CHAPTER TWENTY FOUR

ARE THE GOOD TIMES ON THE WAY BACK?

ORIGINALLY PUBLISHED: NOVEMBER 22, 2016
SHEFFIELD UNITED 1 BURY 0

In my years on the staff here I have seen some pretty strange things. Some of them on the pitch, but we won't go into that - at least not whilst those concerned are still alive! There has also been a few bizarre things off it. We were talking the other day about 'Blades United', which you may recall – that's when the CEO at the time came up with the scheme that fans could actually sponsor the front of the club shirt. I suppose that, as things were not so great around that time, the idea was, in principle, not a bad one. It was certainly innovative for the time; just a little bit confusing in terms of how the packages worked. The concept lasted a season!

You may also recall Desun, the sponsors for the shirt that was worn through a campaign that will be remembered by all for a long time. It was the triple assault season and Desun got some right exposure in that term. The thing was, it was an apple juice drink that you couldn't buy in this country! Strange. When we became a limited company, we did a reverse takeover of a company called Conrad PLC, which meant that we could float more easily on the stock market without the usual period of due diligence. We duly did this and as a result we also inherited a few fairly famous brand names. For a time we owned Le Coq Sportif and also a hospitality box at Old Trafford! Oh, the heady heights of fame.

There have been some classics. You will recall that our gold and purple away kit, the Midas one made by Patrick, which was voted one of the campest ever worn. Clearly no-one saw the pink striped Everton one that skirted under the radar. Now, it would be fair to say that, even though I didn't mind it, it didn't sell very well. We had a director who suggested that, as we needed to shift a few, I was the man best qualified with, and I quote, my 'barrow boy persona' – quite what he meant by that I have no idea – to sell them on the stand concourses cheap and from a suitcase like an old fly pitcher, perhaps?!

Imagine that. You have just paid full whack and then you can buy one for a tenner off some geezer in a sheepskin near the toilet opposite the betting booth. Priceless. It would be fair to say that we still had a few left, stored in the old cricket sheds, or sports hall, depending on your age, that stood at the top of the car park. By this point it had been condemned due to the hot and cold running rats and water – also the asbestos roof may have played a small part.

It was some building though. It had seen some of Yorkshire CCC's greats in the nets, had been used as a water storage tank during the war and now was full of old, wet SUFC paperwork. I don't think that the staff knew how easy you could get in there, but the local lighter-fingered members of society certainly did. Quite soon half of the youth element from miles around were walking around togged up in more Patrick than Kevin Keegan!

I swear that I went up for some old AGM documents and found a kid rooting through a disintegrating box... he had climbed in through a hole in the roof. When I challenged him, he told me the one he had didn't fit and wanted the next size up. Brilliant!

There was also an MD who decided that to save a few bob, the answer was simple; just get rid of all the programme sellers. Yes, I kid you not. We shift a fair old number of the matchday rag and always have done. Much of this is down to Mick Rook-er's ability to sniff out and snatch a ten-bob bit at thirty paces. The other is the sellers. We have had many of them for years and they know what they are doing – Mick also knows where to have them stood and people get used to this. The South Stand regularly has their seller up and down with his shout of "match programmes, three quid" – this is always followed by cries of "how much?"

But again, it's part of the furniture and he shifts a fair few. The first idea would be that people would queue up in the shop or wherever around the ground, now, we all that isn't happening, don't we? You tell that to the MD! In the end, the sellers were kept in a job. The adage about don't fix it if it isn't broke springs to mind, doesn't it? That said, I suppose that you have to try something new at times even if it seems

Derek Dooley's statue at the Lane

a little off centre at first, or just downright mad. That is what makes life interesting, I suppose.

It's all about memories at the end of the day, some stuff you remember as clear as a bell. There are characters that will always be there and always irreplaceable. Derek Dooley always brought a bit of common sense to proceedings back then and that was useful to all. Maybe that is a great example of how things at the club have changed in the last 20 years. Every Friday morning, depending on who was in, either me or Pete Stone would have the job of fetching DD from home and then the rounds would start.

First stop the fishmongers to pick the Finny haddock up; next stop Phillips the butchers on Chesterfield Road for the meat rations for the Dooley household for the weekend. Always ready, waiting and bagged up for collection. Best of all was the bag of hot sausage rolls, Del used to take these around the staff on a Friday morning to have with your mid-morning cuppa whilst the rest of his shopping was popped in the fridge until he went home after lunch. This was a club on the way to the Premier League. I wonder if Martin Edwards or Doug Ellis did similar at Manchester United and Aston Villa?

I doubt it, but they were the little things that used to set us apart back then. A true family on and off the field and, for the first time in a long while, we are heading that way again under a manager in Chris Wilder that will probably remember all of the above about Derek. There will be more memories, of that I have no doubt. Some printable and some not. Either way, it feels like the good times are coming back.

CHAPTER TWENTY FIVE

WARN-ED BY NEIL!

ORIGINALLY PUBLISHED: JANUARY 21, 2017
SHEFFIELD UNITED 2 GILLINGHAM 2

I haven't been banned from many things over the years. I think the first time that it happened to me was from the local Youth club near where I lived at the time. We had a Dansette record player and the club itself had a few up to date discs, the usual chart rubbish of the time including Ottawan (yes, I could do the moves to D.I.S.C.O.), Susan Fassbender (bet you can't remember her) and anything else that could be bought from the ex-juke-box rack at Fred Hartley's on Frecheville shops back in the day.

Kids were also encouraged to bring along their own stuff, and this is where the problems began. I have always been into my music. I missed punk the first time around and began to pick up its finer points in a post-punk sense from older brothers of mates. The Clash were always my favourite, but the Sex Pistols also struck a chord. One of their later singles had an interesting B side that certainly wound older people up with its slightly urban language. This, in turn, made it one of the most spun discs when the kids had a chance to get it on.

The battle was then to have it play until its conclusion. I think you get the picture… after its third appearance of the night, tempers frayed. I wasn't daft, if getting it on the turntable put you up there in terms of street cred then I was in. Enough was enough, young JG was dispatched back down Wickfield Grove with said copy and tail between legs. Sid Vicious had a lot to answer for that night.

The next time was from the Blue Bell at Hackenthorpe. This was a pub that featured heavily in my formative years and I still can't believe that it's now a Costcutter or whatever. It was packed five nights a week and one of the DJs was our very own Gary Sinclair. Now the Bell belonged to Kath and Nev Bradshaw back then and they ran a top house. They also happened to be the parents of Carl Bradshaw (and, of course, Darren and Scott), so this was always a big Blades pub. On my 18th we all met in there to have a couple of beers and then head for Romeo and Juliet's. No game that day, I can't recall why, so an early start was in order.

Kath asked why there was so many of us out that early, she was duly told that it was my birthday. This worked until she was made aware it was my 18th. She barred me there and then. Well, I had been going in there for a couple of years previously. It wasn't wise to mess with Kath. She let me back in a week or so later, but only after a roasting. The third – and so far final – banning came from Neil Warnock and, strangely enough, it also happened on my birthday, though a few years later.

It came midway through what turned out to be a strange season that kind of lost its way a bit as it had done the year before. Post Triple Assault season we had expected so much and yet finished eighth. There had been more changes on the playing side but we had still been a little bit haphazard at times. There had been two great wins over the festive period against Coventry and Leicester City, followed by Wigan beating us 2-0 at home on New Year's Day. As daft as it was, we had then gone to West Ham and beaten them 2-0 at the Boleyn. Highs and lows aplenty.

Soon after we welcomed Brighton and Hove Albion to the Lane. As usual, back then, my matchday duties involved the mascots. Mick Rooker turned the day the kids got into an art form and, when he handed the baton over, I tried to take it a bit further. I think Mick did it for about 16 years, Pete Wigley for a lick before him and then me. It was a full day, in fact, it still is, and we pride ourselves on the time that the kids have.

Now, one of the nice parts of the experience has always been that they get to go in the dressing rooms before the game and meet all the players for a photograph. At a time when tensions pre-match can run high I never ever underestimated the value of being in there, let alone having the freedom from the manager. Priceless, especially where the memories of young fans are concerned. That day, from what I can recall, had run no differently from any other game and we had taken no longer in there than before. It was probably textbook stuff to be fair; we were well rehearsed and knew the score.

If the manager appeared you had outstayed your welcome and it was time for you to do one and get out of the way, sharpish. We had the kids out of the way before Neil appeared, so all should have been good. The game, however, didn't go so well. They beat us 2-1 and scored all three goals. We were awful. Now, in football you are only as good as the last game. Win and the pies are brilliant, beer like wine and programme the best in the league. You are also brilliant at your job. Lose and the pies are stone cold, beer flat, programme awful and the staff are useless. That's the game.

Now the manager was clearly smarting from the performance and wanted something to blame aside of the lacklustre team effort. He pulled me at the training ground on the Monday morning and informed me that the mascots taking too long in the dressing rooms before the game was upsetting the players and distracting them from the job in hand. They had more to worry about and, as a result, from that moment on the mascots would be barred from the area pre-match.

In short it was partially our fault that the team had been awful. I tried to reason with him, but he was having none of it. It might surprise you but Neil can be something of an immovable object when he sets his mind to things. Some might even say stubborn, but it hasn't served him too badly, has it? The proof would be in the pudding. If results improved then it would show that he was indeed right and the regular troop of young Blades were, in actual fact, insiders placed strategically by the managers of visiting teams to disrupt and upset the karma created in the home dressing room. We would see.

The next run of games saw us fail to win the next two home fixtures and I may have pointed this out. The mascots were reinstated for a home game against Rotherham and we won! We had good results in the next few home games and along with the kids, I tried to claim credit for the successes. Although not in ear shot of Neil, of course! The ban was lifted pretty much as quickly as the one I got from the Bell. He laughed about it later and the following season a record number of mascots saw the team promoted back to the Premier League under Neil. I still bump into kids that were knee high and excited back then… only now they are all generally much bigger than me!

CHAPTER TWENTY SIX

OVER A CENTURY OF CHANGE

ORIGINALLY PUBLISHED: FEBRUARY 18, 2017
SHEFFIELD UNITED 1 SCUNTHORPE UNITED 1

Imagine what you have seen in your lifetime. The changes that you have seen, the developments in the world around you. Nothing ever stands still, does it? Think of the changes that you have seen at Bramall Lane in your years. I was first brought to a three-sided ground that had changed little from the turn of the 1900s – if you went for a wee behind the Kop it was in an open urinal that was made out of a pot trough in the floor. The John Street stand was made from wood, the newest side was the Bramall Lane stand and you could park those little pale blue three wheeled invalid cars in the corner of the Bramall Lane stand to watch the game. That was all in the top flight of English football, by the way!

In my years I have seen football from the very top of the old Division One to Division Four and all the way back up and, I suppose, down again. I have seen the South Stand rise over the cricket wicket, the old John Street levelled and the new one (eventually) rise from its ashes as well as the Kop, and indeed whole ground, become a modern all seater stadium… one unrecognisable from the one I first saw with my Dad in the early 1970s. All that and more, and I was only born in 1968.

Imagine, therefore, the changes you would have seen in life had you been born over 100 years ago. A few weeks ago, a man named Frank Wheater passed away in a residential home in Sheffield. I was lucky to come across Frank a few times over the years and he lived a large chunk of his life just a short free-kick away from Bramall Lane on Edmund Road. He was brought into a world of intense change on 3rd March 1914.

Four days after his birth the Blades drew 0-0 in the FA Cup away at Manchester City, nine days after they managed the same score once more at Bramall Lane before finally beating them 1-0 at the neutral venue of Villa Park on 16th March. That year would see us get knocked out at the semi-final stage of the famous competition after another replay at the hands of Burnley. The backbone of the team that played that season would go on to lift the cup, after defeating Chelsea at Old Trafford the following season. Players like Billy Gillespie, Stan Fazackerly, Bill Cook, Joe Kitchen and Jimmy Simmons were mere youngsters, yet went on to carve their names in our history.

Later that year in Sarajevo, on 28th June to be precise, Archduke Franz Ferdinand was shot dead and the world was transformed into a cauldron of war and tragedy, the likes of which had never been seen before. All before Frank took his first tottering Sheffield steps. Frank was watching the Blades at a young age - imagine having seen the likes of Harry Johnson, Jimmy Dunne, Billy Gillespie, Bobby Barclay, Jock Dodds and Jimmy Hagan, whilst being able to compare their skills and flare to that of Tony Currie, Len Badger, Alex Sabella, Tony Agana and Brian Deane? The list can go on and on and change depending on your age and your opinion. Incredible.

He saw World War II break out as the Blades sat pretty at the very top of the old League Division One, prior to Hitler invading Poland and plunging the world once more into chaos for the next six years. Don't forget that the war then came to Sheffield - there had been airship raids during his infancy and his cot would have doubtless gently tremoured to the distant sound of the bombs that

Frank Wheater and family

fell in the east end, searching for the steelworks.

As a nine-year-old, the Blades had gone out of the FA Cup at the semi-final stage once more to a looping David Jack goal for Bolton at Old Trafford and as an 11-year-old, he stood on the streets of the city to cheer Gillespie and the triumphant Blades back home with the FA Cup, snatched from under the nose of the Welsh with a 1-0 victory over Cardiff at Wembley Stadium. As a 22-year-old, in 1936, he saw the Blades once more thwarted in their quest for cup glory in the final against Arsenal, once more at Wembley after yet another semi-final defeat against Huddersfield in 1928.

There were promotions and relegations. The club lifted the wartime League North championship at the end of the war, became the first British club to play in Germany after the surrender and then, in the 1950s, lift the old Second Division championship with a side led by Brook and dazzled by the talents of Hagan. The city changed as well, some by the hands of the council, some by the wings of the Luftwaffe, but the city to which he was born, like the football club, evolved – it really always has, to quote from the documentary back then, been a city on the move.

The City Hall construction was started in 1929 to bring jobs to a city hurt by the depression and was opened when he was 18 years old in 1932. Roads where traffic once flowed freely gave way to pedestrian feet. A big hole appeared in the road and, also in that time, was filled in with the debris from the huge flats that had risen over the skyline when they were pulled down. It was as if both had never existed. Trams went and came back again to the roads and Sheffield United continued to ebb and flow alongside. More FA Cup semi-finals in 1961, 1993, 1998, 2003 and 2014; becoming founder members of the Premier League and clawing our way back. The Division Four Championship and a whole host of other promotions and relegations. Highs and lows

When Frank reached 100, Ted Hemsley went to his party and took him up a signed shirt, it became, for his last few years, his most treasured possession in a life that had seen the first talking films, the first man to walk on the moon, antibiotics, mobile phones, computer technology, the internet. It takes your breath when you even think about those 102 (nearly three) years. Frank passed away within days of his brother last month, and Horace was over 100 as well. I wonder what their secret was? He loved life and he loved his family, his favourite players were names like Hagan, Ringstead, Shaw, Pace, Currie - and that is some compliment when you think about those that he had seen in his life as a Blade.

Our thoughts go to his family as an incredible life is celebrated with his passing… the Unitedite's funeral procession passed through Bramall Lane last week. Working for the club, you see many pass. But this one really got me thinking.

Rest in Peace, Frank.

CHAPTER TWENTY SEVEN

PROMOTIONAL RESCUE

ORIGINALLY PUBLISHED: APRIL 30, 2017
SHEFFIELD UNITED 3, CHESTERFIELD 2
(BLADES WIN LEAGUE ONE TITLE, WITH 100 POINTS)

You don't realise how much you want it until it is nearly there… promotion, that is. As a fan, the last six years have been years of false hope and abject disappointment, scattered with a few bright moments in the cups and now, here we are - back on the road again. The feeling when we plummeted through the trapdoor, under the brief tenure of Micky Adams, was a very simple one. We had been really unlucky and we would bounce straight back up to the Championship; I mean, that was the script wasn't it? We really didn't deserve it, did we?

The reality was very different. We did deserve it and we had been awful for a while. The script for the play-off final didn't quite go to plan and we had the relief of a couple of good cup runs, but even Wembley and the performance against Hull really just papered over the cracks in a sense. We needed to get out of the division. The novelty of going to grounds that we hadn't visited for a long time soon wore off.

Yes, the little real ale pubs that you find in such places are always brilliant and the camaraderie of those that you see week in, week out is really special. The togetherness of the road. But even that begins to wear a bit thin. Let's not mince words, we ended up here because we deserved it in the final analysis. Just none of us expected to be here this long, did we? As I stood with my lads on the stand at Northampton, I felt a mixture of feelings well up.

The first one is always the pride of it all. Our fans are magnifi-

The Blades lift the League One trophy after winning the title

cent; give them a cause to fight for and something to actually believe in and they will rally to the cause and to be a part of it all was special. Chris, Alan and the lads gave a different generation their Leicester, their memory, their promotion carnival. I just felt numb, relieved that we were once more on the ladder up to a better place, a place where we should be.

After the triple assault season I never ever thought that we would be any less than something like a Leicester or a West Ham had been - you know, always upper half of the Championship at the very least. Maybe having a spell in the top flight learning, maybe suffering a relegation and benefitting from the parachute monies, rebuilding and maybe going for it again, ever getting stronger and moving forward.

I was too young to remember promotion in 1971, even though I was there as a nipper with my Dad – I would have been far more into playing tiggy up and down the gap between the upper and lower levels of the Kop and getting a telling off for doing it. All the games at that time seem to merge into one. I really start to have clear colour memories when things started to go wrong in 1976. I was there when Don Givens missed the vital penalty against Walsall and hated him for it - naïve to the last. It was only as I got older and knew players who were around at that time that I realised others bottled it and Tony Kenworthy, who would have been in pole position to hammer it into the back of the net, was sat behind the dugout after being informed by Martin Peters that he was on his way to Forest or Norwich when all was ended and he didn't want to risk an influx of cash by him getting injured. Bizarre when TK went nowhere and became one of the kingpins in the fightback of the following season.

The 1981-82 season was important for many reasons as a young Blade; it was the first season that I went away by myself with mates and braved a wide range of transport to grounds. I loved the football specials and the fact that I don't think I ever paid on one. It was amazing how quickly ticket collectors changed their minds when they opened a door to see a carriage or five full of Blades on their way to grounds. That was the season that the club finally got its ID back and the events of Darlington and, ultimately Peterborough at home on the final day, forged a generation of Blades fans and gave the unique feeling of unity from the terraces that carried us forward.

I think all knew that we would never win the European Cup or possibly the league title, but we had the club back and that was what counted. I know that Reg Brealey gets some stick from some areas about his enforced second spell as chairman, but in his first spell he was inspired and one of the most forward-thinking of his breed in the game. We spent money that even top clubs were not forking out back then and we bought heroes. Keith Edwards, Colin Morris, Keith Waugh – all still heroes of mine all these years on, and for good reason.

The last game I ever went to with my Dad was Peterborough. Dad had stopped away games by and large a season or two before, we needed the money and he tended to work. Home games were always sorted but aways for him were a treat. He always stood behind the same barrier on the Kop, the open end towards the South Stand and, for a change, I stood with him. With ten minutes to go I looked at him to see tears streaming down his face. I assumed it was because we were on the way to the title in style, but later he told me he had cried because he never thought he would see his beloved Blades in Division Four. Stood at Northampton this season, for the first time in my life, I truly got what he meant.

As everyone streamed out onto the turf at Sixfields at the final whistle - in fact, as John Fleck slotted his 88th-minute winner in - tears ran down my face. I was inconsolable and totally lost in the moment. Being a member of staff is one thing, but being a fan is everything and always has been. The tears and feelings were a mixture. The fan delighted, proud and relieved. The staff member grateful of a summer of planning and a period of being able to enjoy the achievement and the chance to finally push on and be the club that we should be again. To me, we have only ever been truly successful as a club when we stop trying to be something that we are not and concentrate on being Sheffield United.

I have seen constant communications and comments thanking Chris for giving the club back to the fans, and I can't argue with that at all. He is, indeed, one of us and always has been - he is what it says on the tin and not one that tries to get the backing of the fans by way of false words and the action of touching a badge that means nothing. He has always lived and breathed the club and wherever he has been in the game, if not in action he has been here cheering on the team. We are living in our own skin again, and it's comfortable to be here. That's down to what he, Alan and Matt have brought back to the corridors.

Having a state-of-the-art training ground and production line is brilliant, but this has divorced the players from the staff to an extent. You never really used to see them over the course of a week because their place of work is up there at Shirecliffe, but that has changed so much. The manager is a regular around the Bramall Lane offices, the players are in and out and, as a result, all are connected. All pulling in the same direction and all know each other again. United is a state of mind and not just a name. United was chosen from the cricket team by our forefathers for a reason. We could have been an Albion, a Wanderers, a City (or a town when we were formed), even a Heeley perhaps, but United was the name chosen.

We are truly being that again, from the terrace to the boardroom, and it feels right, doesn't it? We have some other great memories; the time under Harry Bassett was great to be a fan after a slight post-Porterfield lull and as I said, the scenes at Northampton were, in a sense, a Filbert Street for another generation. I am really glad for them. Both my lads were out on the pitch at the end and waiting for the team to come back out, though I don't think that Chris got stripped down to his pants by the fans. It shows how the stewarding has changed! I waited before I followed them; I just wanted to enjoy the moment from a vantage point and savour the fact that we were on our way back to where I think we should be.

The last few weeks around the ground have been food for the soul. The queues around the car park for a wide range of things have been a joy to see; season tickets, Port Vale, MK Dons, Kell Brook, beambacks, it really is a fantastic time to be a Blade and something we have all waited so long for. To see the coach come back to the car park was special. Its journey up Bramall Lane took longer than trying to get around the anti-clockwise on the M25 on a Friday afternoon; fans spilling out of the Cricketers and the Railway to welcome the lads back to their home, dancing in the road and banging on the windows, again in joy and relief. There have been other times that have been special as I have said and for different reasons, I just think that now really is our time. Time to be us.

I was glad to be there with both my sons, who are both season ticket holders. My big brother was at the Lane watching the game on the big screens in what was a great atmosphere, but, as always,

I wished that Mum and Dad could have been there to celebrate too. But then we will all have had similar feelings about
those who have gone before. I got a text that night from Alan
Hodgkinson's daughter, Karen, to say how pleased the family
were for the club and for Chris for what he had done. 'Hodgy'
worked as Chris's goalkeeping coach at Oxford, right up to retiring at the ripe old age of 76 before he sadly passed away a year
last December.

She said how proud her Dad would have been to have seen
his beloved Blades out of the division and how chuffed he
would have been for Chris. 'Hodgy' always said the Gaffer was
one of the very best and would manage at the highest level at
some point. We loved Alan and respected his point of view beyond measure. I hope he was right and we all want it to be with
Sheffield United.

CHAPTER TWENTY EIGHT

HASSALL FREE

ORIGINALLY PUBLISHED: DECEMBER 26, 2017
SHEFFIELD UNITED 3 SUNDERLAND 0
AND DECEMBER 30, 2017
SHEFFIELD UNITED 2 BOLTON WANDERERS 0

If you had the money, would you want to be the chairman of a football club? You have worked hard all your life, got a few bob and chances are that the family can be comfortable forever, long after you have gone. So why put yourself through it? We have all seen demonstrations across the game when things are not going right. Hundreds jumping up and down in the car park, waving shoes above their heads in protest about the warmth of a pie or the price of a programme when a team loses, yet carrying those in charge high on shoulders when things go right. As someone was once quoted, looking out of the window as the masses raised their cans of Stella aloft in tribute… "In a month's time, they will want me hung again!"

He had a point. This ownership lark is not for the faint-hearted. There have been many chairmen at the Lane, but one that had the unenviable task of steering the club through some very choppy waters indeed was John Hassall. Hassall was a young director when he was asked to join the board in the early 1960s and one that had done very well for himself in business. He worked for the family name of Hassall Homes, one of the biggest local building firms in the area back then and, as a lad born and bred in Hackenthorpe, it was their name that you saw more often than not advertising the new family houses that sprung up over the fields between Mosborough and the rest of the world - as the post-war baby boomers laid down their roots away from the council estates that they had been brought up on.

Dick Wragg with John Hassall

I would imagine it was a good time to be a builder, as over 600 Hassall Homes were flying up each year back then. Totley-born Hassall was a Blade through and through. He loved the club and was honoured when they asked him to join as a director in the days of Dick Wragg and Blacow Yates - a young and successful businessman to lend his skills and, quite often, money, to keep the club afloat.

The club was reaping the keen eye of Archie Clarke, its chief scout, back then. Names like Mick Jones, Alan Woodward, Len Badger, Frank Barlow, Geoff Salmons and Alan Birchenall had come through its ranks to name but a few, and the future was looking very bright under the watchful eye of John Harris.

Our overseas tours were legendary, and one of the directors elected to travel out for the BOAC competition, a tour along with Blackpool, playing games out in Canada and New Zealand over some six weeks. Local lads who had probably previously never travelled much further than Cleethorpes on a school trip now had the chance to travel like James Bond.

So proud was Hassall that every document, no matter how minute, was kept as a souvenir of this life-changing adventure and it gives a fascinating glimpse into what a major undertaking that was in 1965.

The board was a different animal in those days – its purse strings heavily controlled by their ability to guarantee sums of money to the bank and also by the original shareholders of the club who exercised voting rights. After the record sales of Mick Jones to Leeds and Alan Birchenall to Chelsea, the fans demanded that Wragg was 'sent to Vietnam' as punishment. Finances were not good. It was announced that cricket would be given notice to quit its historic home of Bramall Lane and that, over the wicket, would rise for the first time a stand making the famous ground a proper four-sided affair with the sole purpose of football. The quoted amount was £650,000 - a huge sum at that time.

Wragg decided that his role with the FA and FIFA, plus the need for a new direction, saw the need for him to stand down. A new chairman was needed and John Hassall was the man approached. What he found was a mountain of spiralling debts and relentless pressure from the bank to repay its overdraft, almost on a daily basis. His attention previously given to running a successful family business now had to be diverted into the running of a football club that was failing in health. The decision for John Harris to stand aside for the second time led to the quest for a new manager to take United forward and fast.

John was one of the party that met Brian Clough after his departure from Derby County to offer him the job at the Lane. The Sheffield Star's long-serving Blades correspondent, Tony Pritchett, was always given information from Hassall 'off the record' – a trust Tony never betrayed, and this was one of those times.

Clough forwarded the names of the players he would want to bring in to build on a backbone of Woodward, Currie et al and anyone who knows football of the era will guess each name – they all ended up at Nottingham Forest and many of them got a couple of European Cup winners' medals for their troubles.

But the money concerned gave the United board a heart attack and the rest is history. Hassall appointed Ken Furphy and played a part in taking us to our highest post-war league finish, just within touching distance of Europe, and his nights were often spent out on the road with the manager looking at players, leaving family to worry about Hassall Homes. One of his first jobs as chairman was to guarantee £100,000 to the bank.

He needed to bring in new investment and quickly as the club had got to the point where important cheques to employees and debtors had bounced, again. He saw to it that they were honoured. In frustration, he went to the board and said: "If you are not prepared to put money in, resign" – a brave and bold move.

He believed that many of them were there purely as a result of their love for cricket as opposed to football, its loss had lessened their interest and this was compounding problems yet further. He broke new ground by being one of those to tempt Derek Dooley back into football at the Lane as the first proper commercial manager and United became one of the first clubs to look and see the potential of sponsorship, and the income it generated.

But he also felt the remainder of the board was short-sighted as the club looked to reinforce the squad, and found that they would sooner sign two or three cheaper players than the quality that was needed. Hassall saw a deal for Francis Lee torpedoed because of the wages, yet saw them rubber-stamp Chris Guthrie for £100,000 from Southend as he was younger and they were more likely to achieve a sell on from him. Lee won the league with Dave Mackay at Derby, while Guthrie struggled.

Sacking Furphy after a poor run that left us as good as down by Christmas, Hassall appointed Jimmy Sirrel to take the hot seat. Finances were still poor, and Sirrel's record of miracles on a shoestring and keeping Notts County solvent made him ideal. Again, although a football man of honour, his ways were found strange by the players and he never really fitted.

Harry Haslam also had a reputation as a shrewd wheeler dealer at Luton and the deal was done to bring him in with Danny Bergara and David Pleat as coaches - Pleat being the one

Construction work on the South Stand

the club had the eye on as a manager of the future. At the last minute, he stayed at the Hatters, and that plan failed.

Hassall was chairman over the period that saw us make back page headlines as one of the first into the Argentine market following the 1978 World Cup. Much has been written about the Blades and Diego Maradona. The club were offered the teenager and, despite reticence once more from the board, the chairman was keen. Haslam had said that, if they signed him, they could get rid of the other 10 on the field as he would beat them all himself. The story goes that, that night, a Buenos Aires police chief visited Haslam in his hotel room and he was told the player could leave the country when he got his cut from the deal. That ended that.

Hassall's son Paul tells me that as the plane left South American soil, Ricky Villa and Ossie Ardiles were destined to wear a red and white shirt along with Alex Sabella and Pedro Verde - that was until, once more, the board got cold feet about the fee. A friendship with Spurs manager and Yorkshire lad Keith Burkinshaw led to a conversation that saved the Blades' face and saw the Argentines become White Hart Lane immortals as we began the slide to Division Four. Things were so tight that Hassall was sending his own staff to work on the Ball Inn training ground if the boiler packed up or building work was needed. As bills remained unpaid, his bricklayers finished much of the work under the South Stand in an effort to get it open after two years of construction.

The game against River Plate is one remembered by a generation as many of the World Cup winning team played against the Blades as part of the Sabella transfer to the Lane. Daniel Passarella, Mario Kempes and all, it was some night. It gave hope to the Blades for its revival and the president of the famous South American club gave Hassall a beautiful diamond-encrusted pin to cement the friendships that had been made.

The final sale of the dream came when Sabella departed to Leeds. A failed transfer to Sunderland alerted the fact that he could be bought and it was Hassall's friendship with Manny Cussins at Leeds United that sealed a deal for him to follow Tony Currie and Mick Jones up the M1.

So bad was club debt, much of the money owed to local businesses and tradesmen, that Hassall brokered the deal in cash. To make sure that all were paid in full, he instructed the club secretary to write out all the cheques in advance to settle all debts. This duly happened and the bank went ballistic. Those owed money were, according to Paul Hassall, paid.

Finding the situation crippling, he went out to find guidance and investment and found Reg Brealey. In short, Brealey fell in love with the club, bought the major shareholding and began to erode the old school yet further, instigating major change.

Over his tenure he had some major support, citing Alan Laver as a great friend and support to both he and the club. The day the deal was done with Brealey,

Hassall shut his briefcase and left the Lane, never to return. He didn't retain a seat on the board and felt it better to leave and let Brealey crack on with things, as simple as that. As far as his family was aware, he was never asked back.

He had, in essence, married the love of his life, and the marriage went sour due to a fair bit of interference from the family.

Hassall went back to building, frustrated to the end that he had been held back by financial problems and restraints during his time at the Lane. Retirement took him to Andorra to live, but he watched the Blades from afar via satellite or listened to the games over the airwaves. Although he wasn't present at the family parties anymore, he still sent his best wishes.

When Paul Hassall attends games now from the stand he finds it hard to believe that his Dad was once chairman. He was brought up being taken down to the dressing rooms before a game to be hoisted onto Alan Hodgkinson's shoulders and was christened 'brains' by the players, because of his uncanny resemblance to the Thunderbirds scientist due to his glasses!

Paul is still a Blade and fondly remembers being taken to away games, shown into the boardroom at Highbury and touching the FA Cup and League Championship trophy as he walked past them. No camera selfies in those days!

He also recalled being away at Ipswich with his Dad and the team, and as the lads were training on the Friday afternoon the Cobbold brothers invited John and son for 'lemonade' across at the ground. He soon found out this was champagne and that the small round balls being scooped onto crackers on the side was caviar!

"Dad always tried to act with integrity," he recalled. "He would have liked to have achieved so much more, but the circumstances and background at the club stopped that." John Hassall passed away in Andorra about a decade ago and the club held a minute's silence in his memory. My meeting with Paul explained a lot more than I already knew about his tenure. Like I said, who would want to be the chairman of a football club?!

CHAPTER TWENTY NINE

PITCH PERFECT

ORIGINALLY PUBLISHED: AUGUST 5, 2017
SHEFFIELD UNITED 1 BRENTFORD 0

It was truly incredible over the summer to see the ground change before our eyes as the Kell Brook show came to town. Every time you walked up the tunnel to have a gander, more of the famous playing surface disappeared under covering, with chairs and a whacking great stage in the middle of it all. By the time the day of the fight came Bramall Lane had been changed into a boxing venue and another piece of history was well in the process of being written. Sadly, the fight didn't go Kell's way, but a whole different type of supporter passed through our doors - a very different animal to the football fan in every sense, but sport lovers just the same.

People came from far and wide and it would be fair to say that it is an event that few colleagues who worked it will forget in a hurry. Dodging fighters working the pads in the corridors as you head for the loo isn't something you see every day at our place - well, not these days anyhow! We are always looking for different ways of using our historic home. I mean, if you actually use it for what it is there for, you have the biggest piece of land in the middle of the fourth biggest city in the country that, if used for its sole purpose, opens its doors around 25 times per season. It is an expensive little piece of land to run as well!

Our forefathers had the same issues. It's no coincidence that we can count around 16 different sports being played here (not all at the same time) – they were also striving to make the ground self-sufficient and get the maximum use from it. You only have to read the old board of directors ledgers to see just how many people and organisations were after holding their

A pitch inspection at Bramall Lane... before the Desso

events here. Things don't really change that much. The Desso pitch laid a couple of years ago always provokes debate; after all, it was an expensive decision to make, but one that keeps the Lane at the front of the pack in terms of facilities.

It was no surprise that Glen Northcliffe and his team won the award for best pitch in the division last season - it really is top class, as I am sure Chris Wilder and the lads would agree. It also means that these sort of events can be held here and football be played on the pitch virtually days after. The old pitch sloped dramatically over to the corner between the John Street and Kop stands – the new surface is far more level, so I am told. The old pitch also took a hell of a lot more looking after, if the rain hammers down then the new one should still hold up, while the other began to hold water on the John Street wing, over its last decade in particular. The close season was a huge undertaking, stripping it down and having the top taken off. Sand, soil and a complete re-seeding, it had to be started from the beginning every year.

I bumped into a fella in the car park who had been trying to hunt me down for a while. Now his Grandad , it turns out, had a big part to play in Bramall Lane history and also the Steel City's sporting past. His grandfather went by the name of John Emanual Elms. He was born on Christmas Eve 1874 in, and I quote, the Fir Vale workhouse in Sheffield. Now that wouldn't be uncommon back then I suppose, but in this instance his parents actually ran the place. Just imagine the hardship and poverty that he would have seen growing up.

It seems that he must have been a pretty handy cricketer because he achieved what so many would love to and never get - he batted for Yorkshire in 1905. He began his career with a duck - not the best start for a fledgling career I will grant you - but his second innings, against Derbyshire at the County Ground, brought back a score of 20. A big improvement on nowt! Elms played for the county second XI as well from 1899 to 1906, so he clearly had talent. A Sheffield lad through and through, it was probably no coincidence that he found himself coaching cricket in the nets of the game's natural home, Bramall Lane.

After retiring as a coach, he kept his ties to the Lane by becoming a groundsman. I would imagine that it would be alongside Tom Parkin and his knowledge of the famous wicket would, I am sure, have made him a natural in the job. In fact, he was on the staff at one of the most crucial times in our history, and that was when Adolf Hitler tried to remodel the ground with bombs! Now, it's here where me and his grandson disagree.

Grandson John has some superb photographs, the ones that you have never seen before. He believes that it shows Grandad and his colleagues working on the pitch to make repairs after that fateful night in 1940, and I can see his point. It's a great shot of lads grafting, all in their regulation flat caps, of that there is no doubt. For my money, they are installing drains in the pitch, so I think it's a little before the war. If you look at houses and shops on Bramall Lane behind the old stand, they look in good shape, the night the bombs dropped it wreaked havoc on the whole area, and I can see no visible scars.

Another picture shows them actually laying pipes, again, in front of the Bramall Lane end of the ground – I believe that the man in the hat staring down at proceedings is the man himself. John Jr. could be right, then again, so could I! Let's just agree that they could be repairing the damage or installing a piece of modern engineering that, back in the day, was as ground-breaking and useful as the Desso pitch is to the club of today in terms of helping get more use out of the pitch.

The clear up from the Kell Brook fight was huge, but not as big as the one our forefathers had to do during the war. Isn't it fantastic that these sort of photographs survive? Showing a different ground, a different time, a different world. A window into someone else's life and their history that plays such a big part in what we have become today.

CHAPTER THIRTY

IF I DIED TOMORROW...

ORIGINALLY PUBLISHED: MARCH 13, 2018
SHEFFIELD UNITED 2 BURTON ALBION 0

I am sure that we all have moments in our lives that will stand out and remain vivid until the day that we die. Those moments that make us the people that we are, that set us apart and make us individuals. We all have our own histories. When anyone dies, much of that tends to die with them. We all remember some of the tales that Mum, Dad, Nan, Grandad and whoever told you when you were younger, but how many times do you stop during a day and wish that they were still here to tell you again? Many times, for instance, when something good happens to me or the kids, I think "I must ring Mum and tell her." Sadly, I can't, but wish that I could.

The same with Dad, what a life. A childhood living under the sight of the stands at Bramall Lane, earning tickets to watch United by doing any menial jobs that he could around the ground for cricket and football. He served his country during the war with distinction, but seldom talked about it, except the humorous stuff, and I wish I could remember more of that now. It seemed stale and boring when I was 10, but I could listen to him all night now. He was at the 1936 FA Cup final when we lost to Arsenal and I would give anything to know now how he felt on the day, what the journey was like, the atmosphere, the colour and noise, the game in general. Anything.

I was lucky to know two players that pulled on the famous red and white shirts that day via the work I do for the club. Jock Dodds and Ernest Jackson both lived the dream. I listened to both of them for hours over endless cups of tea talking about every aspect of the final. Jock was the best man for Tommy

Johnson and he married the day before the team went down to London for the game by train. Imagine that. A wedding and a cup final inside 48 hours!

Both now sadly long gone, they did what any Blade would love to do. They stood in the tunnel at Wembley Stadium wearing the famous candy stripes in one of the biggest games that any player could ever contemplate playing in. The fact we lost is another matter - both said that we shouldn't have and that Arsenal were lucky that day. I also knew Albert Cox, another Blades legend, and used to pop and see him when he was alive and well and living in Brinsworth. A proper Blades hardman was Arthur and the man who was dropped from the final after having a fine game in the semi against Fulham. Teddy Davison made the decision to play Wales international Bertie Williams instead and both Jock and Ernest told me that it cost us the game. Williams, it seems, froze, and the problems were compounded by the fact that our skipper, Harry Hooper, was injured early on and in the days before subs, Albert was the 12th man and sat on the bench watching things unfurl. I've seen the pictures and it has to be said that he was looking good, wearing a huge overcoat with a suit, shirt and tie. Not the usual attire on the

David Seaman pulls off THAT save in the FA Cup semi-final

bench at Wembley, unless you are the manager, of course!

These tales were a privilege to hear, and I never got tired of them, a unique VIP seat in the memories of names that are part of the very foundations of our great club. Again, like Mum and Dad, I wish they were around still to hear them all again, a million times. My time at United has given me plenty of those moments as well, I have been really lucky to have been a part of what I would say are some of our greatest moments of the last 60 years. They are stories that I suppose I have also told many numerous times to a great many people, and why not?

To me, one of the best displays I have ever seen from a United side in a major game was in the 2003 FA Cup semi-final against Arsenal at Old Trafford. The minute the draw had been made for the game, Manchester United were on the phone, offering Neil Warnock the use of their Carrington training ground in the lead up to the match and being generally extremely accommodating to us with everything – I suspect that it could have been a little to do with the fact that we were playing the club that was, at that time, arguably Sir Alex's biggest rival.

Our entire operation was transported over the Pennines; commercial, ticketing, the works. All staff on duty stayed the night before and we were in their ticket office at 8am to make sure we were ready. The Gunners turned up late and were all at sixes and sevens, but we weren't. I am proud to say that we were super slick. Manchester United delivered breakfast to us under silver serving domes with their compliments, whilst our rivals didn't even get a slice of toast!

I looked after the mascot, who happened to be Amy Warnock, and as we were guided around the ground we were told that they could not be taken in the dressing rooms without permission of the manager – I must admit that having the manager as the mascot's Dad was a big help here! Whilst I sat having a cup of tea, chatting to Stuart McCall for half an hour, Amy had her pictures taken with the lads – our Arsenal opposite number was fuming in the tunnel!

Myself and photographer David Pye even managed to get out on the hallowed turf. The noise our lot were creating in the

Stretford End was incredible and we soaked up every voice as Amy had more pictures taken. My moment came in the tunnel as the teams came out. I wasn't worried about the stars of Arsenal, the team I was brought up supporting, the team my Dad and grandad supported. Our captain, Rob Page, winked at me and made me feel 10 feet tall. I was there, I was part of it all, and I wanted to recall every second. I walked out of the tunnel behind the players and out onto the pitch as the Blades created a noise akin to a thousand jet engines firing up. The hairs stood up on the back of my neck. Nick Montgomery turned to me and his face was something I will never forget.

The game didn't go our way and, let's face it, it should have done. We were magnificent that day and it took one of the greatest saves ever seen to keep us at bay. We showed class beyond measure and showed to the watching world that the Blades could live with the big boys. I left Manchester sad but proud. Michael Brown gave me his spare shirt that day, and it hangs on the wall of my eldest son's house. After Old Trafford I knew what people meant when they said that, had they died the following day, they would have died happy. Thankfully I am still here and thankfully there have been many other moments since. I hope there are many more before the final whistle is blown.

CHAPTER THIRTY ONE

A BIT OF A MAYOR

ORIGINALLY PUBLISHED: AUGUST 26, 2017
SHEFFIELD UNITED 3 DERBY COUNTY 1

There are many images and aspects of last season that will live with me forever. It's not always easy being a member of staff and a lifelong Blade. When it's good then it really is amazing, and the day at the Town Hall was incredible. From the moment the open top bus turned up in the car park, the reality of it all really began to sink in. We had waited a generation to see us lift a major piece of silverware. We had a bus when we went up to the Premier League in 2006, a fantastic achievement, but we were given something that looked like a large tea tray as reward. I'm not knocking it, and it is useful in the office (only joking) but this time we had a proper cup - even if the Gaffer did try to throw it over the front of the bus on Surrey Street!

I doubt that any of us really expected as many to turn out as they did. It was incredible as myself, Dave McCarthy and Pete Stone walked the bus up from the ground to the Town Hall. It took nearly an hour longer than we thought it would as we fought our way through the crowds down the Lane and up into town. There was a blockade outside the Cricketers that held us up a bit - amazing what bar stools and a sign that looked suspiciously like it had been 'borrowed' from the Bramall Lane upper concourse can do to hold a coach up.

The other thing that surprised me was the number of Blades that insisted on walking up with the coach, it was like the Jarrow March. Truly amazing scenes and plenty of familiar faces. Nice to see them with something to smile about for the first time in a long while as well; a real carnival of red and white that night. As a kid, I used to get dragged each year by Mum to watch the Lord Mayor's parade. Does it still happen? I remember thinking that it just looked like a fleet of rather grubby lorries that had been done up to look like cheap versions of various other modes of transport, basically advertising local businesses. Plenty used to turn out for it, though, didn't they?

Clearly, in the Town Hall, the manager took a fancy to the Lord Mayor's rather nice hat and I thought it suited him, but the colour didn't really go with his eyes. It ended on the heads of one or two of the players and staff before the Lord Mayor, Denise Fox - who took it all in good spirit - finally got it back. She did well... I suspect that there were plans for it to accompany the team back here. Still, at least she managed to hang on to the chain of office! Without any disrespect to the Lord Mayors of this great city, like their parade which seems now to have gone, I am never totally sure what the role is, or what it does. I know that they work tirelessly whilst in office to promote Sheffield and local charity and that can never be a bad thing, but I wonder whether it carries the same weight of office that it used to do back in the day?

I am sure that, for those who have put that chain on, it is one of the key moments in their lives, a bit like winning the cup I suppose, and I get that. I'm just not sure a modern generation is in tune with the role, a bit like the parade. The day also reminded me of a book that I picked up many years ago, and that is the yearbook of one of Denise's predecessors, Alderman Alfred James Bailey, who was in office in 1924/25. Someone rang me and offered this fabulous thing as it was being disposed of. I couldn't believe that no one would want something as beautiful as this.

Leather bound and gold embossed, it is an accurate and, in all honesty, loving look at a year put together by what seems to be their press officer at the time. Now, there have been many United connections with the Town Hall down the years. Alfred Cattell, a famed local fruit and veg merchant, was chairman of the Blades from 1930-33 (the first to witness relegation from the top flight) as well as Lord Mayor. His association with the club lasted 40 years and his brother was also a director.

George Marlow had a turn in both roles of office and the magnificent Clegg family played a key part in the development of the game of football as well as having a father and son put the chains of office on. I don't know if Alderman Bailey was a Blade, but he was certainly a very busy man in his year. The press cuttings describe his journey as being from ploughboy to chief magistrate - quite a journey.

Not from Sheffield (he was born in Scredington in Lincoln-shire) he had arrived here as a youngster and, a bit like Dick Whittington, had found the streets were, for him anyway, paved with gold. From a first job as a drayman he became a staunch trade unionist before becoming a surface worker at Treeton Colliery. His leadership and views saw him become of-ficial organiser of the National Union of Labour and also the first district secretary of the National Union of Municipal and General Workers. There was no silver spoon here; a labour man through and through.

In newspaper reports, he described himself as being a "born fighter who had fought for many causes" – he said that, in his term of office, he would "fight for the city of Sheffield". Stir-ring talk indeed. The book shows he and his consort attended hundreds of events. At Christmas, they toured the hospitals and the socialist Lord Mayor was still not shy to speak out on behalf of the working man from his position of office. His secretary has pasted the many formal invitations to events into this work of art. Importantly, his year of office saw Sheffield United win the FA Cup Final at Wembley on 25th April, by a Fred Tunstall strike to nil.

There are plenty of press cuttings of the cup run, but, best of all, there is a great sepia shot of the legendary Billy Gillespie being handed the cup by the future King George, as a clearly delighted Lord Mayor looks on in the Royal Box. The menu from the celebration dinner at the Royal Victoria Hotel is also there to remind how good the food was that night! He is quoted as say-ing, in the local press: "It was the first football match I have ever seen, and I thoroughly enjoyed it."

Hardly a lucky mascot through the rounds, but he sat and

watched the game with the current Queen's Mum - it was the lady herself who handed the winners medals out. The Duke famously said to our captain "I believe this is yours, Mr. Gillespie" – I wonder when a member of the Royal Family will say that to a Blades captain again? He sounds a fascinating man, I like his principles and the journey he made from humble beginnings, and I love the book of his term. He looks a formidable man. I doubt that John Nicholson or George Waller tried to pinch his hat when then team arrived on the Town Hall steps in 1925!

CHAPTER THIRTY TWO

CUP OF CHEER

ORIGINALLY PUBLISHED: MARCH 17, 2018
SHEFFIELD UNITED 0 NOTTINGHAM FOREST 0

I seriously doubt that, whatever I see or do in the future, I will ever live through anything quite like the events of the end of last season. Some fantastic memories. As a Blade, I always kind of resigned myself to the fact that we wouldn't be winning a European trophy any time soon as I was growing up. Being a Blade was never about that. It came through Dad and wasn't a choice, it was a part of your birth right. It was what I was always going to be as it was for my big brother. It wasn't about challenging for a championship season in, season out. It was about my club, our ground, our history and heritage. As Chris Wilder says often… a proper club.

I remember us missing out on the title as a kid. Too young for it to really hit me then, but I recall the misery in the house when we surrendered our top flight place a short time later. Dad had given up when Jimmy Sirrel took charge. He said that we should have been looking to change things, bring someone young and ambitious in. Despite a proud background at Notts County, Dad saw Jimmy as a football dinosaur and also a lack of ambition from the board. At least my brother could take me if Dad had lost heart. He wasn't away long, by the way.

The pain of that era is well documented. There was the odd bright moment as we slid into the mire of the Fourth Division, but the season that followed that is one that galvanised a generation of Blades and brought the club back to the fans. We got our heroes and a championship trophy to go with it - we also got our self-respect back and a foot on the ladder once more. It was so important.

Keith Edwards, Tony Kenworthy, Colin Morris and all the others, you could play football in the school yard again and not be content with being Paolo Rossi or Kevin Keegan. You could be a Blade again with your held higher than ever. In a football city, that is an important thing when you are growing up. What Chris, Alan, the backroom staff and the boys did last season was give another generation its Leicester, its Darlington, and that happened on that hot afternoon in Northampton. Never thought a town famous for its shoes that gave the team its nick-name of the Cobblers would come to mean so much to me and every other Blade – Cobblers, the day was not. It was unforget-table, and I shared it with both my sons – they had no choice either!

It kind of drew a line under that historic season last week when the EFL contacted us to say they would be collecting the League One trophy. So many memories are attached to it for us all. I have had the pleasure of looking after it since it was handed over to Billy Sharp at the end of the last game against Chesterfield. I have polished it, displayed it in the museum and also had the honour of taking it out and about to local schools over the past months. There was something really special about putting it in its box in the boot of my car, taking it to a school, setting it up on a table and then, after doing a presentation on the Blades alongside Tony Currie, unveiling it to the gathered kids.

We did assemblies with as many as 350 kids in it and it al-ways amazes me at that age that, whatever their allegiance in terms of club, the language of football translates so easily where silverware is concerned. The reaction that it got from all was truly brilliant. The stunning thing is that, when you ask kids who they follow, there are still far too many in the city that will tell you Manchester United or Chelsea. I appreciate that parents can move to the city from all parts of the country and, indeed, globe for that matter, but Sky sometimes has a lot to answer for.

We gave sets of tickets out as prizes during the sessions, and so many of those who got involved have had the chance to come and see the Blades for themselves - many for the first

time. I hope that they all enjoyed it. There is no substitute for football in the flesh is there? When the league picked up the trophy, it was like saying goodbye to a friend and so many memories – in fairness they live on in the mind, and in pictures from the day and all the events that followed on. I hope who-ever lifts it high at the end of this campaign gets the same buzz from it that this club has - it lifted us higher than anyone could have dreamed of after so many false starts and crashing disap-pointments. It became a symbol of what belief and bonding can bring to a club like us. As Darlington and Leicester did, it sig-nalled a return.

The good news is that, even though the real thing has gone, to prove that we were there and won it, we get a full-sized rep-lica to keep as our own! In fact, when we stood them side by side the replica is actually a little bigger, if anything. It's always been the custom to do such things. We have a replica of the original FA Cup that we lifted in 1899 and, despite being com-pletely accurate in every way, its tiny compared to the one that sits in the National Football Museum with our name on.

Whereas the one that went back last week had its handles picked out in gold, this one is all base silver, but still looks mightily impressive. Better than I think any of us thought it would or could be. A fitting reward for a historic season for us all. It also means that we can carry on with the work we have started in and amongst the schools in and around the city, and we will be doing that as soon as possible.

It's incredible also to think that the replica we now have will stay at Sheffield United long after I have gone, as a last-ing reminder of the fact that we are one of the few clubs to have lifted every division in the English game. A testimony to the rapid change brought around the place by Chris Wilder. In the same way that I get our little FA Cup out of the cabinet for ground tours now to talk about the feats of Foulkes, Needham, Bennett and Co., I hope someone in the future talks about Billy and the boys on 2017, keeping their names alive for future Blades to learn about.

The contribution that they all made to the history of the club will last the test of time and I, for one, am proud to have been a small part of it all. At one point the trophy sat on my desk in the office as we got pictures of all the staff with it. It was the best paperweight I have ever had and the photo I have with it is one of my most prized possessions. Along with the one a 14-year-old JG had with the Fourth Division championship, which seems a lifetime ago.

CHAPTER THIRTY THREE

YOU DRIVE ME CRAZY

ORIGINALLY PUBLISHED: NOVEMBER 21, 2017
SHEFFIELD UNITED 4 FULHAM 5

There are so many cars on the road these days that it is frightening. I had a car as soon as I could drive – I have always been obsessed by them, I have owned more than even I can remember and still can't resist looking, even when the one I have is perfectly OK. Dad didn't have a car until he was about 35. It wasn't that he couldn't drive, the fact was that he just couldn't afford to buy one in post-war Britain. The first one was a 1948 Ford Prefect that cost £100 - it was black, and my big brother sat in the window of the house on Springwater Drive all morning on the day it was delivered.

Mum looked as though something nasty had been wafted under her nose, she wasn't too chuffed with his choice. To make matters worse, when she sat in the passenger seat she disappeared in a cloud of stuffing via the huge hole in the front. Apparently, all the time he had it they went through a succession of passenger seats, none of them matching the colour of the others in the vehicle!

Dad's second car was a newer Prefect, but this time in green. All was well until the paint started to need touching up, then dad's legendary colour blindness rose to the surface. By the time they got rid it looked like an army staff car, camouflaged! People don't realise but Sheffield, at one point, had a fairly healthy car production output itself - not on the levels of Ford, Austin or any of the big boys, but still a fair few. From 1900 through to around 1930, companies like Hallamshire, Cavendish, La Plata, Stringer, Richardson, Charron and the fabled Sheffield Simplex were well known and respected names.

The Johnson family... real Blades legends

Simplex were some cars, made in the steel city between 1906 and 1922. Hardly any survive, or at least are known to. The company started in London and had the distinction of wealthy local landowner Earl Fitzwilliam being one of its directors. He decided that the company would have a better future building cars in Yorkshire and offered land he owned at Tinsley to bring the company to Sheffield and create valuable local jobs, and this is what they did. The Simplex was no ordinary car. For a start, they were dearer than a Rolls Royce, and, as a result, they were never built in huge mass-produced numbers - this means that there was a pretty good list of customers for future records, bear in mind that you would have had to be worth a few quid to have bought one in the first place.

A few were owned in the city, and some were exported out as far as Australia and Russia. The most famous one was owned by Lord Riverdale and had been on display at Kelham Island Museum. Another one belonged to Norman Adsetts for many years and, I believe, is still in the area. Two were made not that far from the Lane. HFG were based on Broadfield Road by C.

Portass and Son, who started out making optical and scientific instruments when they first formed in 1889. During the first World War they began to make munitions and wing sections for the Sopwith Camel aeroplane and decided they would take the skills they had learned in that trade to make a small lightweight car.

It was probably too ahead of its time and was classed as a 'cyclecar' – it was air-cooled as opposed to water. They ceased trading in 1921, but part of the company remained as the Heeley Motor Company, making its own bodies and fitting them to other company chassis. Charron Laycock had a good six years building cars at the Laycock works on Archer Road at Millhouses. There was one of these in the reception of the firm for many years that I recall as a kid. Richardson - who had two years from 1919 to 1921, building their own marque - started in a garden shed on Holmhirst Road at Woodseats before moving to better things a stone's throw from the ground at Napier Street. There is a surviving example, again at Kelham – all this going on around the Sheffield area.

Not many players these days in the first team don't have cars. I can think of one who uses the train and taxis, but he shall remain nameless! As a kid, when we used to go up to the Ball Inn training ground or wait around the players' entrance on John Street, I could tell you the player by the car. This was a team at the top of the English game and not a Ferrari, Maserati or Aston Martin in sight back then. The most exotic was the purple Trevor Hockey Triumph with the fur bonnet (it's true, ask Grandad). TC had a Ford Cortina 1600e like my dad's, Len Badger had a Ford Capri, Alan Woodward had a Marina 1800 TS and John Flynn had a Triumph 2000. I may have got the odd model wrong but the makes are all spot on!

The thing was that these players had the same car as your dad, no big hitters. I remember being quite impressed that Dad had the same sort of car as TC back then, but that was the way of the world – they still lived next door to you, on the same estates. Well, not on the Scowerdons, I grant you, but you get my point. Sabella drove a Scirocco a little later.... I know because the club still have records for his unpaid parking tickets! When it was Len's testimonial, he drove around Sheffield in an old Austin Cambridge painted up in red and white with his shirt number on the bonnet and doors to attract attention. That was until the local constabulary pulled him over for driving an unroadworthy vehicle!

A few years ago, in the programme, there was a feature about players and their cars, including striker Ashley Ward, but by then, things had changed. Going back, we think the first United player to have a car was our record goalscorer and member of the Blades family elite, the Johnsons. There is a great picture of Harry Johnson with his father and team mates sat in an open top car outside the same players entrance on John Street sometime in the early 1920s. Harry was one of the real stars of his time and from a family that, between father and two sons, played a major part in virtually every honour won by Sheffield United.

In that one car in that shot are five FA Cup winners medals from Johnson, Boyle, Johnson and King – not a bad haul. And not a fur bonnet in sight! Harry set the standards in many ways for the club, but I bet he never thought that his first car would pave the way for the clutch of Mercedes, Audis and so on that we see today. I wonder what he would think?

CHAPTER THIRTY FOUR

YOU DESERVE A MEDAL...

ORIGINALLY PUBLISHED: FEBRUARY 10, 2018
SHEFFIELD UNITED 2 LEEDS UNITED 1

When I first started on the staff at the Lane, there was a big old safe in the strong room that was used for the turnstile money after a game. At the bottom of it was a steel drawer that was just full of odds and ends that had just accumulated over the years – the kind of stuff that becomes worthless but had a value to whoever had the keys to it back in the day. Always curious, I had a dig around one day and found a few old medals in a freezer bag. All gold, I read the inscriptions and found that they had been won by a real club legend – the one and only Fred Tunstall, of the Blades and England.

Most of them were local competitions - the Senior Cup, the County Cup - and all beautifully made. One of them, however, stood out. The design on the front looked like two old time footballers holding a ball and leaning against a shield. The back was inscribed: 'F. Tunstall – Sheffield United – English Cup Winners'. The penny eventually dropped that the English Cup was once the more popular name of the FA Cup, so there, in my hands, and kept at the bottom of a safe, in a plastic bag, was the medal awarded to the man who scored the goal that brought the cup back to Bramall Lane for the fourth time, the last time, so far.

This was handed to the player after he walked up those famous Wembley steps and shook hands with the woman who we would one day know as the Queen Mother. The medal was also the starting point of what would become the museum collection here. The club had bought the medals years before from his daughter, and it seems that no-one really knew what to do

next. Thankfully Derek Dooley and Kevin McCabe liked my idea and I was given the chance to build the fabulous collection that we have today.

It also got me thinking. Why would anyone want to sell their family jewels? If my Dad had won such a gong I would not be able to part with it, but I began to learn that the further it gets down the line in terms of generations, the less relevance it has. There are also times when players, who didn't earn the money that is around today, needed to give some financial security to themselves and their families, and I do get that. I mean, how many of the boys of '66 have sold their World Cup winners' medals for such a reason? There are always two sides to every story. I would say that I know the whereabouts of pretty well all of the FA Cup winners' medals awarded to our players in 1899, 1902, 1915 and 1925 – there are a couple of exceptions that I suspect may have gone abroad at some point, and also a couple that have been lost to time.

Charles Sutcliffe is perhaps not the most famous or illustrious Blades goalkeeper ever, but he was good enough to win a FA Cup winners' medal against Cardiff City. He hailed from Bradford and his eldest brother played for England at both rugby and football. Charles made his name and won a West Riding Senior Cup winners' medal with Leeds City; when they were wound up for financial irregularities in 1919 he was one of the players who found himself in the auction to repay funds, and ended up at Rotherham County, having a few good years with them. He was brought in by the Blades to cover a goalkeeping crisis caused by the sacking of England and FA Cup winning player Harold Gough and the retirement, through injury, of the reserve 'keeper, Ernest Blackwell. Incidentally, Gough had upset United's staunch Methodist directors by buying a pub in Castleford - hence the sacking. In the 1925 FA Cup run, Sutcliffe saved a penalty in the semi-final at Stamford Bridge against Southampton and was good enough to keep a clean sheet against Cardiff - not a bad reward for 53 games in a Blades shirt. He lost his medal off his watch chain, never to be seen again, whilst bagging sand for the effort in World War II. Joe Kitchen was a United great of his time. Signed from then-league club, Gainsborough Trinity, and born in Brigg, he was only 17 when he made his Blades debut.

Apparently, he just missed out on an England call up in 1909 and was back on form, playing in the 1914 semi-final against Burnley and then scoring the third goal in the 3-0 rout of Chelsea in the 1915 FA Cup final. He netted a very impressive 169 goals in 342 Blades outings and when his career was over, had a pub in the market place in Barton-on-Humber called the Wheatsheaf – fascinating as he was a non-smoker and teetotal! There were reports of his death in the early 1960s, but then he popped up talking about football and Sheffield United on Radio Humberside over a decade later! He finally passed away in 1974 in Enfield, his precious medal passed to his grandson, who worked at BBC Television Centre in the sports team.

He had told colleagues for years about the footballing talents of Grandad Joe, rightly proud of him and his FA Cup exploits. Many took it with a pinch of salt, so he promised one day to bring the medal in to prove he wasn't lying. The day came, and he set off for work from the home counties first by train and then by tube, checking all the time that the battered little purple leather case that held the family treasure was safe and sound in his pocket. He got off the tube at Wood Lane, crossed to the famous building and made his way to the office. As the crowd gathered, he reached in his pocket and took out…nothing.

The pocket was empty! Despite his endless checks and due care, the most precious thing in his life was gone. Appeals, searches, ads in the press and on the news brought nothing back. Somewhere between Kent and London on the transport network, and lodged in some dark crack or crevice, is probably still a 1915 Sheffield United FA Cup winners medal. One lost did come back. Walter 'Cocky' Bennett had two FA Cup winners' medals, a runner up effort and a host of other caps, shirts and gongs from a glittering career.

His tragic early death from a mining accident in 1908 saw one of them pass to a nephew, the 1899 one. He wore it on a watch chain everywhere and, whilst climbing a wall to get access to a Blades game at Leeds Road, then home of Huddersfield Town, he lost it. The medal slipped from the ring suspension and was lost. Again, despite appeals, it was gone, seemingly forever. Many years later, when workmen were renovating the stand, one of them saw something gold glittering in the muck and dust, and there it was.

Credit to them, they traced the family and re-united it with the unlucky owners' descendants – a happy end if ever there was one. It is now on display where it should be – the Legends of the Lane museum at Bramall Lane. I tell you what, the bloke who found it and traced the Bennett family really did deserve a medal for that, didn't he?

CHAPTER THIRTY FIVE

PAINTING THE PICTURE

ORIGINALLY PUBLISHED: AUGUST 22, 2017
SHEFFIELD UNITED 1 LEICESTER CITY 4

Around 10 years ago, it was decided that the old boardroom in the South Stand had rather had its day. The idea was to make it a more modern place with its own restaurant, offering fine dining, a new directors' suite and a new boardroom at the opposite end of the stand to where it had been for many years. Now, I liked the old boardroom. It was exactly as a football boardroom should be. It had a lovely oval table with a green leather top and matching old school carver chairs around it. I believe Derek Dooley bought it from a chemical works at Staveley when it shut down and it really looked the part.

There were oak display cabinets at one side that had all the pre-season trophies in there, lightly dusted with, surprisingly enough, dust! This was largely down to the fact that someone over the years had lost the cabinet keys! There were England caps in there won by former Blades and the blankets dished out to the ladies or older guests in the directors' box. It all had an air about it - if you got summoned to the boardroom you upped your game. To get there you had to go through the sponsors bar, past what, at that time, were the offices of the chairman and the chief executive. You then had to wait at an ante door that led to a short corridor past the directors' guests room and to the seat of power itself.

That boardroom had two very unusual features, added by former chairman Reg Brealey. The first was a bed, which pulled down from the wall just in case he was marooned in the Steel City or just couldn't be bothered travelling back to Lincolnshire. Not a bad extra! The second was a concealed hatch that meant if he was cornered in there for whatever reason and couldn't get out of the main entrance, he could slip through, down onto the South Stand concourse, out around the ground and through John Street. Escape made easy!

There were several pictures on the walls. The main one was commissioned from Joe Scarborough in 1989 to commemorate our centenary; a beautiful thing that still hangs in the modern boardroom today alongside its 125 counterparts. The other was an oil painting of one of Sheffield football's true early pioneers, WF Beardshaw. Beardshaw had played for many of the local sides and had trialled for England. He had the nickname 'Baltic' as that was the name of the factory he owned in Attercliffe, the Baltic Works. He had been a major figure in the local game for years, and one of those who had stood out and against the rise of professional football as opposed to the amateurs.

He had been a key committee member of Sheffield FC for many years and had stated that, in his opinion, the pros playing the game in Lancashire were 'wicked' and that the legalisation of paying footballers would tend to lower the game of football. Really strange, that being the case, that years later he would be one of the founding fathers of the Blades! It was he, along with David Haigh, Joe Tomlinson, Joe Wostinholm and Harry Stones, that formed the cornerstone of the meeting that took place on 22nd March, 1889 at 10 Norfolk Row, along with JC Clegg, that led to the formation of the club that we know today. Before that he had played a part in launching the famous amateur club Corinthians and served on its first committee, so his credentials were beyond compare.

I've never really been sure who gave us the picture, it is a lovely thing of what looks like a very kindly old man. I used to get great pleasure in telling schoolkids on tours that his eyes followed you around the room. Scared the living daylights out of them, it did – I'm sure 'Baltic' wouldn't have approved of that! Now, when the renovations of the boardroom were done, it was decided that most of what was in there had to go, table and all. As a historian, I was dead against it, but it was pointed out that the old-fashioned styles and worn look of the furniture

The old Bramall Lane boardroom

and cabinets, along with the old-style gilt frame and appearance of the picture, just didn't go. So into storage they went, to be forgotten about.

Now, football can be a very superstitious place, but I had never really stood back to look at how the club had fared since our founder father was bubble wrapped and placed under the stairs in the dark. That season ended, of course, in relegation. There was a couple of attempts that failed in the play offs, but the fortunes remained very much the same, mixed to say the least. We had other bad luck – key people close to the very heart of all things Sheffield United passed to a higher division, though it would be ridiculous to think that mortality rates were affected by a piece of canvas. But it still covers the same time period. You kind of got the feeling that we were jinxed.

Finally, last summer the fans got what they had been need-ing. A manager that was one of them. It was fairly common knowledge that, had Chris Wilder not been playing or managing somewhere else and we were playing, he would be sat next to you at the Lane. Finally someone who understood and got just what it was like to be a Blade, the hopes, the fears and expectations. It didn't work out over the first four games, but anyone with half a brain knew it would turn, we just needed to settle down and, as Dave Bassett often said, get a rub of the green. That bit of luck that turns a game and gives you something to build on and move forward. Just after the fourth game I was searching for something when there, under the museum stairs in a small storage area, I came across old WF.

Other stuff had been placed in there and on top of him; in fact, there were now little bits of damage to the painting itself, but not in bad shape for his age. Even I had forgotten he was there. I suppose I felt guilty that someone who had done so much for us had been neglected in that way, so I decided to unwrap him, dust him down and let him look out onto Bramall Lane again from a wall in Legends of the Lane. After all, it was the least I could have done.

We all know that things began to turn from us in spectacular fashion. It seemed as though WF coming out of hibernation had changed things. In reality, it was the manager, coaching staff and players that found their gear and flew with a style and flair that will set that season out, as the years go by, as the one where we became truly United again and played with a passion on the park that fans truly signed up for.

That said, when WF came out, we started winning. Everyone deserves a helping hand and my superstition now means that he has pride of place permanently back in Legends of the Lane - and will remain there. I now don't think his eyes follow you - his expression is one of happiness to be back.

A bit like us.

CHAPTER THIRTY SIX

A DAY NOT TO FORGET

ORIGINALLY PUBLISHED: APRIL 10, 2018
SHEFFIELD UNITED 2 MIDDLESBROUGH 1

It seems like a lifetime since I first got involved with writing for the club. I can't really remember how it all came about, but I first wrote the beginnings of my usual ramblings around the 2000/2001 season when the museum project started out. Like most jobs at the Lane, it was just a case of being asked to do something and cracking on with it. The first thing I did away from the club was eight pages in the FA Cup final programme when Chelsea played Arsenal at Cardiff; the reason was that, at that point, our former striker, Jock Dodds, was the oldest surviving FA Cup final player and the last still breathing from the 1936 final.

The FA liked what I did and asked me to do a bit more for a free day out at the game with my eldest lad and one that I will always recall. We were a part of the Arsenal contingent before, during and after which meant that we really got a taste of what it was like to lift such a thing, and were made so welcome. The first book that had my name on a cover was one that I wrote with a friend and Blade who had already done some real quality work, and has done many more since – Gary Armstrong.

We would meet for a few beers when he was in town and I would relay some of the fantastic tales about players and games of the past that I had picked up during my work. It was there that the idea for 'Sheffield United – The Biography' came from. I learned a lot from Gary about how you had to go about things when it came to writing, I just thought he was being a bit harsh on me when it came to the demands of what he wanted, deadlines and so on. I was naïve and took a lot of it the wrong way at the time, but, with hindsight, it was a valuable lesson and I am pleased to say that the friendship survives to this day.

Also, when I look back at it now, I realise how proud I am of the book and the part that I played in its birth. It was a club commission and sold out - in fact, I think it is one of the biggest selling books we have ever done and, even though it now is a little out of date as a decade of history has gone between, I think it still looks stunning.

Coincidentally, at the time, Tony Adams had been involved with Gary through his lecturing. The former Arsenal captain is a really intelligent lad who had re-written his life after a few scrapes as younger player and was also then assistant manager to Harry Redknapp at Pompey.

Adams was a colossal player, and one that I always really admired. He matured into a fine skipper for the Gunners and a leader on the pitch for England. I remember the game at Cardiff against Chelsea was his last - Arsenal and Adams were brilliant that day and as the champagne flowed on the pitch, the man who had publicly and honestly battled addiction stood back and let his team mates enjoy the moment and the triumph. I think he said that he did not want the risk of one drop of booze touching his lips in case he was tempted to take the bottle and finish the lot. Straight and to the point.

Gary had told Tony about the book, it had just come out and Pompey were due at Bramall Lane in a Premier League game. As ever, that day, I was out on the pitch with the sponsor tour doing the usual history lesson and souvenir pictures when, out of the tunnel and on to the pitch walked Tony Adams, heading straight for our group. I walked over and asked what we could do for him and, bizarrely, he asked for me; Tony wanted one of the books and Gary had pointed him in my direction.

I was happy to sort him a copy out - in fact I was more than a bit made up that he was in the slightest bit interested in a book about my beloved Blades. He offered to pay for it, but I insisted that I was having none of that - we still had a couple of the complimentary ones left that the publisher sets aside to distribute around members of the press, and as far as I was concerned one of those was very much his. He still insisted on some form of payment and I was having none of it - a deal was struck that I would take the book down at the end of the game to the away dressing rooms to make sure that he had it for when they set off.

Now, at that time, we had a lad working matchdays for us who had also gone through his own personal struggles and 'Addicted' - the book that Adams wrote - had been a real source of inspiration and comfort for him over a bleak time. He had approached me and asked if, as a favour, I could ask Tony to sign his copy for him. Now, usually, we don't do that sort of thing as it's not our style to bother and harass, especially when you are a member of staff. But on this occasion, and knowing the background of the story, I asked if Tony would be in a position to help.

Tony asked me what the issues had been and how he was dealing with things and, after listening intently, he told me that he would not be travelling back by coach, and that his car was parked in a bay to the back of Cherry Street car park. His instructions were simple: when the team coach had set off, just wait, he would be out 10 or so minutes later. He told me to ask the lad to meet him quietly at his car to sort things out, which I duly did.

At the end of the game, I took the book down and once again turned down the offer of money. My eldest lad looked after mascots back then and was with me. Tony asked him if he played football and, if so, what position? As he was a goalkeeper, Tony disappeared and returned with David James, his match shirt and a pen. A dumbstruck Liam stood there whilst an England 'keeper signed away and handed it to him, something he treasures to this very day.

At the end of the game Tony Adams met the lad, signed his book and then sat talking to him in the car for over an hour about what he was going through. He ended by giving him his mobile number, with the instruction to ring him any time he felt like straying from the path – what a man. What reminded me of the above is that last week David James contacted the club to ask for our assistance over a project on football ownership he is doing, and I was more than glad to help.

It also gave me the first chance, a decade on, to thank him for that gesture he made to my lad. He will have given a thousand shirts away in his career and signed a whole lot more stuff, but it meant a lot to me to show how much it was appreciated. A decade or more on it still meant the world, as did the gesture of Tony Adams to someone he had never met before who faced the same demons as he did. Neither played for the Blades but both are high up on my list of favourite players.

CHAPTER THIRTY SEVEN

LOST IN TRANSLATION

ORIGINALLY PUBLISHED: APRIL 28, 2018
SHEFFIELD UNITED 0 PRESTON 1

We have had our fair share of foreign players over the years. I was watching a great programme on ITV4 the other day that showcased the influx of players from overseas into the English game, and it was great to see Alex Sabella get a fair bit of coverage, along with some nice footage of him being introduced to the fans at the Lane, coming out of the old John Street tunnel in his nice beige flares. As ever Ossie Ardiles and Ricky Villa got the headlines, but we were the first and Alex was some player - he certainly grabbed this 10-year-old's attention and enthusiasm when he put pen to paper.

Prior to that the most exotic player we probably had was John Cutbush, because he had been born in Malta, but the overseas players began to make their mark from that point on. Our lads also found themselves having the chance to go over and play in the States. Our former secretary, Keith Walker, had gone over there as one of the game's top dogs and soon players like Alan Woodward, Eddie Colquhoun and Colin Franks were off to try their luck on a different continent. You may have seen footage of the legendary Pele scoring a screamer for New York Cosmos, only to have Tony wrap himself around him in celebration! Bizarre.

I suppose we really cracked on with foreign players a bit later than most and it was Harry Bassett who finally began to change things when he brought in Norwegians like big Jostein Flo and Roger Nilsen. The Scandinavian market was still largely untapped at that point, and we did OK. There was Jonas Wirmola and we also had Tore Andre Flo on trial. A bit later we

Vass Borbokis celebrates against Sunderland

had Brazilian-born striker Marcelo, when we were not short of a good frontman or two – Jan-Age Fjortoft was around at a similar time.

Marcelo was a lovely, polite lad. Very switched on as well - his missus was and probably still is a solicitor - and he could also play a bit. Most remember the FA Cup game at Coventry when he scored the equaliser and ripped his shirt off to reveal... another shirt. Don't think I have asked him how or why, I should have done as his English was better than mine! Petr Katchouro was also around that time, the 'Menace from Minsk'. On his day he was brilliant, but when we signed him the Belarusian international could not speak one word of English, and that can sometimes be an issue when the wind is howling around your ears at Abbeydale. Then there were the Greek lads, they were a bonus and maybe slipped under the radar at the time. Like many, I didn't know too much about Vass Borbokis until that first home game of the season against Sunderland.

His transfer had been negotiated by Howard Kendall just before he departed back to Everton once more and finished by Nigel Spackman. What a player he was, scoring on his league debut and being more or less ever present before being injured in the FA Cup game against Cardiff City. He asked then manager Steve Bruce if he could return to Greece to recuperate and was apparently refused, he went back anyway and was fined and placed on the transfer list.

You will remember he went to Derby and we got Jonathan Hunt and Rob Kozluk in exchange. I'd just started on the staff then and, as I bit of aside, I took ownership of Vas's club car, a nice black Mitsubishi Carisma!

Traianos Dellas was the other Greek lad. He was a big unit and not long after putting pen to paper he needed back surgery, which that held him back a tad. He was more versatile than a Swiss Army knife and played for us in many positions when he got his chance – he blasted a screamer of a goal against Portsmouth from about 40 yards and also got two in a 3-2 loss at Tranmere when he came on as a sub. Now, I can't recall why he went back. Some said it was homesickness, I seem to think that he also had to either finish or start his National Service as is the custom there. Either way, he went back and gained his first full international cap in 2001.

You don't need me to tell you that he did OK for himself. A few may recall that he joined AS Roma, and he helped Greece to a surprise win in the European Championships in 2004. Tri was another lovely lad, so was Vass, but as they both returned home to Greece and the world kept on moving, we lost touch with them both fairly quickly. A couple of weeks ago we played

Nottingham Forest, and I was behind the scenes waiting for the teamsheets to be ready when a tall, smartly dressed guy came up and shook my hand.

I sense that, from the blank look on my face, he knew I hadn't the foggiest idea who he was! His name, it turned out, was Michael Anagnostou and he is now the head of football operations at the City Ground. It was more alarming that, as we talked, he clearly knew who I was, what I did at United, the approximate time I had been here as a staff member and also the names of a fair few of my colleagues. Then the penny dropped. Michael had been the interpreter for the Greek lads and had been around the club to help them out back in the day. It was then that I remembered him. I mean, it was almost 20 years ago. It turned out that he had been in the professional game back home before the new owners took over at Forest and, as he had already spent time here and had a good understanding of the workings of an English club, he was the perfect choice for his role!

It also turned out that he had kept in touch with both of the lads. Vass is coaching at the AEK Athens academy and doing well, Tri is also still in the game. We shook hands and swapped numbers as I wanted to get hold of them both, and a few minutes later he shouted me over. On the phone was none other than Big Tri himself, and it was great if not a little surreal to catch up with him after all those years.

We now have contact with them both and I will do a piece next season. Tri asked me to wish all at the Lane his very best and to thank the fans for making him so welcome during his time in the Steel City, so I've done that. I wouldn't argue with Tri – have you seen the size of him?

CHAPTER THIRTY EIGHT

LIFE'S A BALL, BOY

ORIGINALLY PUBLISHED: FEBRUARY 20, 2018
SHEFFIELD UNITED 2 QUEENS PARK RANGERS 1

As a kid it was always one of my ambitions to be a ball boy at the Lane; it looked just the job for me, although not for a game against Leeds – I would imagine that got a tad warm for any of the poor souls having to fish the ball out of the away end. I remember meeting Billy Bremner at a football do once. I wanted to take an instant dislike to Don Revie's midfield general and skipper, but he really was a top man and spoke warmly of the Blades, until the subject somehow got around to the dark arts of Bramall Lane's ball boys.

He pointed out that if United were losing and there were 15 minutes to go, there would be more ball boys on the cricket side of the ground than you could count on two hands, and they would sprint en masse to get the ball back to a red and white shirt and back in play as soon as possible. If, however, the Blades were in control of the situation there would be one solitary figure who would slowly trudge over the vast expanse that was the famous wicket to get the ball back to a white shirt at some point before the end of the season!

Now, it would be unfair of me to comment on this accusation, especially as the great man is no longer here to reply, but he thought it

JG with Chris Morgan

was funny, a great tactic and one that many a side fell foul of under the same circumstances. I just regard it as gently playing to our strengths! Many a Blade will have been a ball boy here as a young 'un and quite famously a United fanatic called Chris Wilder cut his Bramall Lane teeth doing that very job. I wonder whether there have been any other football club managers who have gone from that role to player and then on to gaffer?

Speaking of famous ball boys, I'm told that during a Barnsley against Blades match in the 1990s, a Friday night fixture, a Tykes goal was celebrated by a ball boy behind the goal – it was none other than future Blades legend Christopher Paul Morgan! Apparently, there's TV footage to back up this claim.

I never realised, until recently, that to be a ball boy, you could apply back in the day to the club secretary. In my day it seemed like the secret service, it was only ever those who played for Junior Blades or Sheffield Boys that got the gig. But it would seem there was a little more leeway, certainly when Arnold Newton was in the hot seat.

A few weeks ago a fan dropped a postcard in at the museum that backed this up. Keith Kukuc was a Woodhouse lad, born and brought up there, and had done the ball boy's job before when the Blades met Sunderland in 1966, standing guard in front of the Shoreham Street Kop. The date was 5th February and the Blades drew 2-2 with the Mackems, the goals being scored that day by Gil Recce and Barry Wagstaff.

The game made a big impression on him, and he obviously did a decent job, as when the testimonial game for club stalwart Cec Coldwell was announced, he received a postcard from the club inviting him to report to the players' entrance on John Street at 6.30pm on Monday 31st October 1966 to act as a ball boy for the game against an All-Star XI.

Great club servant Cec was one of the nicest blokes that you could wish to ever meet. Snapped up from Norton Woodseats for a grant to them from United of £100, it would prove to be one of the best buys imaginable. Joining in 1951, he went on to captain the club when we were promoted in 1961 and formed part of what is regarded as one of the greatest defences ever to play for the Blades. Generations were weaned on the line up of Coldwell, Shaw, Shaw, Summers and Richardson, in front of goalkeeper Alan Hodgkinson, and for good reason.

A total of 477 games in a red and white shirt tells the story, and Cec was skipper from 1957 before handing duties over to the legendary Joe Shaw. His last appearance for the club was the only time in his entire career that he ever appeared as a substitute. In fact, Cec was still registered as a player until 1968, but by then he was working as a junior coach. John Harris promoted him to the role of first team coach in 1969 and he had two spells as caretaker manager. He was involved with the club until the days of Ian Porterfield and respected by generations of playing staff.

For his testimonial, the crowd of just over 10,000 is strange; it really doesn't seem to reflect the esteem that he was clearly held in by club and fans at all. I can see no real reason as I look back as it was just a few days after a 3-1 win over West Ham in a season that would see a respectable tenth position secured in the top flight. I can imagine that Cec was disappointed with the size of the crowd, and quite rightly so. That said, a young Keith had a night to remember. He recalls the ball looking as though it was about to go out of play and, as he moved towards where he thought it was going to go, 'Hodgy' told him to get out of the way of it!

For the evening Keith had bought a new pen and autograph book in readiness for the Blades and All-Star team to be signed up as a real schoolboy trophy. Sadly, the pen never got any further than Ken Mallender, who swiftly pocketed it after signing his book, never to be seen again! 'Hodgy' had chatted to the ball boys during warm up, Keith asked him what he thought of the Sheffield city coat of arms badge that had become a feature of the kit a short while before and the legendary 'keeper informed him that it was 'rubbish'!

The night saw the Blades draw 5-5 with two goals from Reece, one from Woody, one from Charlie Bell and one from Tom Fenoughty. All good exhibition stuff. Keith now lives in Spain, enjoying retirement, but is still getting back over here a fair few times a season to watch his beloved Blades. He has given the postcard over to the club museum and we thank him. Somewhere he also has a letter from the club and the autograph book. All great memories. But no pen!

Chris Wilder – the former ballboy who went
on to live all our dreams and more!

CHAPTER THIRTY NINE

RESERVED OCCUPATIONS

ORIGINALLY PUBLISHED: JANUARY 30, 2018
SHEFFIELD UNITED 0 ASTON VILLA 1

Remember the days when the reserves very often played at home when the first team was away, or even on a regular basis under the floodlights at Bramall Lane? When my big brother wouldn't or couldn't take me to an away fixture, the alternative was often an afternoon with Dad at a ressies game. I well recall a fan having an opinion on events which he vented over the top of the old concrete dug outs for a fair old while - long enough to finally test the patience of the legend that was Alan Hodgkinson.

Then on the coaching staff, Hogdy left his position, walked up into the stand and picked the advisor up by his lapels to politely ask him to shut up and keep his vast wealth of managerial experience to himself. Now, as someone who knew 'Hodgy' pretty well, I can testify that he had hands the size of shovels, the handshake of a silverback gorilla and, when he drew his 5ft 9in frame up to its extent, he was an imposing figure to say the least.

It would be fair to say that when Alan finally put him down, at the behest of Billy Hodgson, his new 'friend' was quiet for the rest of the game! The reserve games were also some event under the floodlights, and we used to pull some fair crowds back in the day - especially if there were a couple of big names playing, or a favourite making their way back from an injury or illness. I can remember a huge crowd playing the others here when Brian Deane had been out for a while, possibly when he had that bout of glandular fever. I seem to think that David Hirst was also doing the same for those across the city that night.

As a staff member I also remember with sadness Dane Whitehouse's knee telling him that his time was up in a game one evening at the Lane, that was one of those nights that you never forget, and all for bad reasons. He went in the dressing rooms, took off his boots and said: "That's it, I'm done." To try and carry on could have seen him in a wheelchair and the cost for him was too much. No-one could have wanted to come back more and no-one could have been more a Blade.

Dane Whitehouse, aka Sid

Dane, or 'Sid' to those who know him, could have gone to several clubs and earned a lot of money for his services, but he was one of that breed who just wanted to play for his club and do his best. He worked himself to the limit to get back from what happened against Port Vale, but it was just too much. No one could have done more and all the staff that worked with him that are still here respect him beyond measure, but that was a tough night.

When Ron Reid was in charge of our youth set-up he could tell a tale or two. He never quite made it as a Football League player, but his reputation in non-league as a player and manager was formidable to say the least, and the standards that he set at Shirecliffe bore much footballing fruit for the club. He told me that, as a young 'un for Chesterfield reserves, they were down at Bramall Lane one Saturday. In the United side were several greats coming to the end of illustrious careers, one of them being the giant that was Joe Shaw.

A young and confident Ron walked from the away dressing rooms to the tunnel to find the legendary defender was captain for the red and white wizards and stood, majestically, holding the ball under his arm in readiness. Ron introduced himself, full of youth and confidence and looking forward to trying his luck against one of the best defenders of the era. What an opportunity for him.

Joe held out the ball. "Have you seen one of these before, son?" he enquired. Ron took the bait.

"Yes, it's the matchball, Mr. Shaw," he offered.

"Well take a good look son, it's the last time you will see it this afternoon!"

Ron told me that Joe's prediction had been correct. Joe ran the game as he had done in a record number of Blades games, and Ron got nowt for his troubles that afternoon! Despite my love of all Blades history, I have never been the biggest programme fan. The really old ones are fascinating, but I never liked the rigmarole of lugging them around after a match. Too much hassle for me. I always read other people's though… they are the cheapest ones!

It, therefore, surprised me that, when sorting out a box of my rubbish at home the other week, I found a reserve team sheet from August 1985. A miracle that has survived because I have trouble locating my birth certificate and driving licence most of the time! I'm not even sure why it has survived to be honest, but it was great to look at the players we had on display that Wednesday evening all those years ago, against Leeds United for a 7.30pm kick off. The referee was Barnsley's Steve Lodge, who did quite well for himself.

Paul Tomlinson, who was always a steady pair of hands, was in the net and Kevin Arnott, one who never did much wrong for me and made over 150 first team appearances for us, both played, as did Brian Smith, who was a desperately unlucky player as a Blade. I remember going to Brian's testimonial game one Bank Holiday Monday - a local lad who had the chance but not, sadly, the luck. Lee Walshaw played too. I have known Lee for many years and he is currently doing a sterling job guiding the huge project at Bramall Lane that is the future of ladies football.

The number nine that day was my all-time hero, Keith Edwards. All have their own opinions about football players, but to me he is the most naturally-gifted goalscorer I have seen in a red and white shirt. After we had been on the rocks as a club, he was one of those who helped us get back on track and re-gain our dignity – he meant the world to my age group and still does. For Leeds, the name that really sticks out is Terry Phelan, a player that had a good career spanning over 400 league appear-ances as well as 42 Republic of Ireland caps around the time that Big Jack Charlton made them something of a force to be reckoned with. He also famously made his mark as a member of the Wimbledon Crazy Gang and pocketed an FA Cup winner's medal in 1988.

He spent a time with us in 2001, playing all of the first six games before losing his place to Shane Nicholson! A few names from that night, and I still can't work out why the hell I kept the team sheet. It must have been my love of goal-king Keith. By the way, I know a Blade who had a tattoo to celebrate the club winning the Pontin's (reserve) league a few years ago, but that's a different story…

HETTY BIRTHDAY TO YOU!

ORIGINALLY PUBLISHED: SEPTEMBER 27, 2017
SHEFFIELD UNITED 2 WOLVERHAMPTON WANDERERS 0

I have told the story many times; I don't do birthdays. Most kids at 15 get a new BMX or clothes but I got my Dad in a pine box as it was decided that was the day of his funeral. Funny thing is, as I have grown older, it hasn't got any better. Every birthday therein has been greeted with a certain lack of interest from me. What becomes clear, especially from our records, is that people are living longer. Our database has an unbelievable number of fans who are getting to 85 plus.

Last week I was invited to a special birthday party and it was a real privilege to be even thought of. As one of the longer serving members of staff and also the one who historically has dealt with our former players, I have been very fortunate to get to know some truly great names from the past, and still count many of them as close friends, as well as their children and, in some cases, grandchildren. We keep in touch with our own – that's how any family should be.

I never saw Joe Shaw play, but all those I know who did tell me he was one of the greatest. Dad said that, and I always appreciated his view on football. He knew his stuff. I got to know Joe through the cub, and spent many happy hours in the company of him and his missus, Hetty, at their place in Dronfield, transfixed by his stories of bygone days and of great days gone by. Magical - and always treated as a friend, something I never forgot as a young 'un on the staff. I was always very proud to tell people he was a friend and even 10 years after his passing, that feeling never changes.

I asked Alan Hodgkinson about him on many occasions. I

mean, who would be better placed than the man who played behind him in the legendary defence for so many games? 'Hodgy' told me that he never saw him flustered and that Joe always seemed to know exactly where the ball would be and, as a result, he would always be there. His timing and anticipation were truly breathtaking, as was the way he would coolly bring the ball down and play it out of trouble. 'Hodgy' described him as being the first sweeper in football without knowing it. High praise indeed from another legend, wouldn't you agree?

When Len Badger made his debut against Leyton Orient, one of his first touches of the ball was to hoof it down the pitch and out of danger. He felt it was the right thing to do until a clip round the ear and the warning that "I don't know who taught you that, but we don't play football like that here son" convinced him that Joe's way was the way forward! Joe went to a higher league many years ago, and he is sadly missed by us all, but the surprise birthday party was for his wife, Hetty, and I was there to celebrate her 90th birthday. What a landmark.

All had been hush-hush, I don't know how Pam and Yvonne (their daughters) managed it. The club sent a beautiful bouquet on the day itself, and the Senior Blades had also made a huge fuss [Hetty attends every week]. On the Sunday, we all had to be at the Green Dragon in Dronfield for 1pm – the cover was that she was being taken for dinner. When I got there the room at the back was already full and there were some names that read like a Blades "Who's Who".

Back then, the players really stuck together, as did their families. Jean Ringstead was there, wife of Alf of Blades and Republic of Ireland fame. Beryl Shaw, wife of Graham, was sitting with them. Ringstead, Shaw and Shaw... how much would they be worth now? Soon, Tommy and Connie Hoyland arrived – it was also Connie's 85th birthday that very day.

They both look fantastic and what a club servant Tommy was, also a good landlord when he had the Sheldon - as was Graham and Beryl at the Sportsman just down the road. Mick and Glennis Jones were there, along with Len and Mal Badger. Hard to imagine that they both took their professional bows in the same team as Joe, bearing in mind he made his Blades debut in 1944.

As all-time appearance maker, Joe's football career spanned a generation. Mick and Len both refer to him as 'fatther' (yes, with a double 'T') – a term of endearment for the influence he had on them and the way they were looked after by the older players. Mick is rightly lauded for his exploits at Bramall Lane and also for what he achieved under Don Revie up the M1. Len is a Lane legend and our youngest ever league captain. Tony and Elizabeth Currie were also there, as was former 'keeper Paul Tomlinson.

All were there for Hetty. She had no idea of the surprise. To be fair, even when she entered the room she didn't twig until she saw Mick Jones and the penny finally dropped. I have Jean Ringstead, Beryl Shaw and Hetty on that they must have done a deal with the devil, because none of them ever seem to age.

Hetty cuts the cake on her 90th birthday

They all look fantastic, and it really is something when you see them all sat together, along with Connie Hoyland, nattering away and having such a good time.

Think of the changes they have seen at Bramall Lane. In their day, after the game, women were not allowed in the snooker room where the tea and sandwiches were laid out for the players – they all used to huddle In the doorway of the ice cream factory opposite the players' entrance on John Street, waiting for them to come out at the end.

No lounge or bar, just the wind and rain of Sheffield on a 1950s winter night waiting for the heroes of the Bramall Lane crowd, before getting on a tram home with the fans. I have always referred to them as the 'Golden Girls' and for good reason.

There is a reason why they are all still friends after all of these years and a reason why Mick Jones, Len Badger, Tony Currie and all were there – these were the people who put an arm round them and made them feel part of the United family when they were youngsters.

That's why they all still have a tie to the Lane today. Happy birthday Hetty - you and the girls were the very foundations on which Legends of the Lane were built and the power behind the throne. The unsung heroes at a time when football and the world was changing. We raise a glass to you.

CHAPTER FORTY ONE

THE BUMBLIES

ORIGINALLY PUBLISHED: DECEMBER 29, 2018
SHEFFIELD UNITED 3 BLACKBURN ROVERS 0

How many pairs of twins have played for Sheffield United at the same time? Go on... have a think. Well, I can only think of one set, and they were as Sheffield as a bottle of Henderson's Relish. They were regarded by many as amongst the very best in the Steel City at that time in their age group and also rubbed shoulders in the red white and black with some of our greatest ever names.

They went by the name of Robinson and were from the Wybourn. George and Bill grew up on Maltravers Road and were Blades through and through. In fact, that area of town produced some cracking players back then. Charlie Bell joined United and David Ford went on to have a great career across the city and at Newcastle United before coming to Bramall Lane.

The twins both played for the school team and were selected for Sheffield Boys - an honour and the hallmark that you was a cut above the rest. At 14 they were playing in the same side as lads two years older without any difficulty at all, and that would eventually bring the scouts looking. Surprisingly, neither sadly made the step up to the Yorkshire Boys level. When the trials took place the manager only put forward defenders and mid-fielders and, as both played up front, that seemed to be the end of that.

Around that time a figure came into their lives who helped shape some of the greatest crop of young talent that Sheffield United has ever seen, and his name was Archie Clark, head scout for the Blades. George and Bill signed as schoolboys in 1963, coming in to train on a Tuesday and Thursday at the Lane under a staff led by the legendary John Harris, assisted by John Short and Harry Latham.

There was some talent at the club straining at the leash to get through into the first team. Alan Woodward, the Wagstaffs, Len Badger, Mick Jones, Alan Birchenall, David Munks, Ken Mallender, Mick Heaton and Phil Cliff were just some of those that went on to realise that dream. Older Blades fans will confirm that they were quality players. You could sign an apprentice contract at 15, and both were offered terms, such was their progress. If a club didn't offer you a professional contract before your 18th birthday then that was that.

"It was a great life, and we loved it," remembers George. "We had to sweep the stands, clean the first team boots, balls, toilets... Whatever needed doing, we did it." It was about this time when they had a nickname bestowed on them that has stuck to this day. Alan Birchenall decided to call them 'The Bumblies'! "It was because he said that you couldn't tell one bumble bee from the other," laughed Bumblie one, George. "We never minded it, it was given for the right reasons by a mate and that is what football is all about. Good craic and a lot of friendship."

Some of the senior professionals could be hard taskmasters, George cleaned the boots of Graham Shaw, and he had to make sure they were spot on. At that time, players like Joe Shaw, Doc Pace and Alan Hodgkinson were all-powerful. "At times we felt like slaves with the work we had to do for the senior players, but to us they were legends and had done all of the same things themselves as they were growing up," George said. "We just got on with it and felt lucky that we were in the position we were in."

Sadly, neither were offered professional terms at United. Bill departed first and was snapped up by our neighbours over the city for a spell. Brothers who had always been team-mates found themselves pitched against each other in the Northern Intermediate League Cup at Bramall Lane on 16th March 1965; Bill in the same side as Graham Pugh and Sam Ellis, George with Barry Wagstaff, Frank Barlow, Munks and Cliff.

Not long after, Bill's career as a football player was all but over. Wednesday didn't offer him a contract, and he was out in the big wide world. Football back then never prepared you for what would happen if you didn't make it in the game. When you were out you were out. John Harris was a gentleman, and, via director of the club, John Hassall, he set him up with job on their sites, and that was a big help. George, too, was about to taste disappointment. John Short called him over and told him that the manager wanted to see him in his office.

The kind Scot explained that he would not be offered a deal as other players were, in all honesty, better suited to the professional game at that time. Just the luck of the draw when you come through at the same time as players like Jones and Birchenall. Still wanting to help, Harris informed George that he had set up a meeting with him for the following day over at Doncaster Rovers with manager Bill Levers. Seeing it as a real olive branch, George set off over there by train and made his way to Belle Vue, then home of our South Yorkshire neighbours.

George got the same chance as Bill had been given at Hillsborough; six months to see if he had what they wanted and that would take him up to the magic age of 18. "It soon dawned on me how different it was from United. At the Lane, even as youngsters, all our kit had our initials on; socks, shirts, shorts, the lot. You always knew that you were wearing your own stuff," remembers George. "At Donny it was a free for all, you got what was going and what there was generally wasn't great. I suppose we had been spoiled." Sadly, George wasn't kept on and his life in professional football ended on his 18th birthday. Some present!

Life on the outside saw him take a job as a pipe lagger, whilst still turning out on a Saturday for Windsor British Legion and on a Sunday for a side that dominated all back then and for many years, Arbourthorne EA. Both a decent standard that attracted many others who had diced with the career of a footballing professional; he was in good company. A bad knee injury saw George have to wait some nine months for a cartilage op. "That was what the national health was like then. Over that time I clapped loads of weight on and lost a great deal of fitness.

There was then a hell of a long-time recuperating." As footballers, the twins were both finished at the age of 25.

George added: "It was all so different back then. When we were at United, we used to play games on the local fields on a Sunday afternoon against friends like Wilf Smith and David Ford, who were both Wednesday, and Charlie Bell, who was at the Blades with us, would play too. Imagine what any manager of a top-flight club would do today if they found their players doing that on a Sunday!"

George attended games at the Lane as a season ticket holder along with his son Paul; he still does. Sadly, Bill passed away six years ago. "We both gave it our very best shot in football, but our best back then just wasn't good enough. We got a lot of attention as youngsters in Sheffield because we were twins, but I would like to think we could also play a bit. I am proud to have played for Sheffield United and also to have been in the same team as so many great names that went on to become United legends."

'The Bumblies' are remembered with affection by them all. Every time I see Mick Jones, Birch or any of them they always ask after George because he was a mate and they remembered the good times that they all had together. I think George does himself and his brother a disservice. You only have to read the clippings in his scrapbook to see how highly they were both rated. You then also see how fickle the football finger of fate can conspire to end a career in the same way as it can make one. They were two of the best of their time in this city and stood shoulder to shoulder with their team-mates on the same level.

And they were good enough to sign for the Blades.

CHAPTER FORTY TWO

TOILET HUMOUR

ORIGINALLY PUBLISHED: DECEMBER 26, 2018

SHEFFIELD UNITED 3 DERBY COUNTY 1

Brentford, last month, was pretty standard in terms of away games in London on a Tuesday night. We had a reasonable journey down to the smoke whilst the heavens opened and when I say reasonable, I mean as reasonable as any journey to the smoke can possibly be viewed for a midweek game. For years I have just travelled with the club. It's easy for me; I can do my work until the last minute, leg it up the car park and jump on the coach. Keith Firminger is one of our stewards, and he is always kind enough to save me a seat.

We have had some interesting times at Brentford, I recall a night game when all the coaches got back to Watford Gap before being turned back by the Metropolitan Police. It turned out that after the game a Bees fan had sadly died, and they believed it was as a result of trouble between fans. The days of CCTV would now have shown that the unfortunate lad had a fit and had gone down, hitting his head on the pavement edge. This didn't become evident until all had got back to London and were promptly turned back north. We arrived back in the Cherry Street car park at about 7am!

Last month, we arrived at the parking place at around 4.30pm and made our way to a nice little pub on the other side of the ground by the name of the Black Dog. Nice ales, food and half a coach of wet and weary Blades were made to feel welcome. We swam back to the ground at 7pm as the roads were by now flooding nicely, finding our seats in the upper tier in plenty of time for the game. Now, it would be fair to say that the loos at Griffin Park aren't the best, and the queue that met me halfway up the stairs had persuaded me that the best time to check out the porcelain would be when the match had started. Common sense in my book.

As proceedings got underway, I decided to keep the cork in as long as I could to avoid asking fans to let my ample frame past as they are trying to watch the game.

I had also been able to catch up with a fair few London Blades, whose company I had not had the pleasure of for a while. Brentford forgot how far most of us had travelled and had the gall to score the first goal. In fairness, they must have realised because they were good enough to score an own goal as the equaliser shortly after. At this point my bladder was beginning to squeak a little, so I decided that 1-1 was a good point to pay my first visit. It took a while as I bumped in to a few of the usual loyal travelling faces that you see at every game come rain, shine, division and results. Finally, I arrived at my destination just in time to hear the roar go up as Ollie Norwood crashed in what will possibly be a contender for goal of season next May.

As I raced back, zipping up my flies and drying my hands on my coat (of course I had washed) something occurred to me. How many times have I made such a journey to watch my beloved Blades and missed either an absolute barnstormer of a strike, or an important decision or event that has changed a game? How many times has the need to answer the call of nature lost me a moment of celebration or golden Blades memory? It's easily done. At the semi-final at Wembley in 1993, my then-missus had employed the same strategy of letting all get settled before nipping off to spend a penny.

In her absence Chris Waddle was lucky enough to score what I can only describe as a fluke of a goal past the towering presence of Sir Alan Kelly. Her return to the seat next to me found myself and a good few thousand others with heads in hands. She asked me what was wrong, and I just looked at her in disbelief. Then she said: "Have we scored?!" Well readers, I think you can all guess the measure of my pithy and witty reply to that one. She finished off by pointing out that there was no need for my manner as it was "just a game". Enough said about that then!

The game that, for me, illustrates just how the call of nature can destroy a football dream actually took place in the inauspicious surroundings of the Withdean Stadium, then temporary home of Brighton and Hove Albion FC. The Withdean mostly consisted of temporary stands built from scaffolding poles - one side of the ground had a huge pub and, if you were nice to the bouncers, they actually let you in through the back doors to save you having to walk around. Nice people. Now, on the way down my recollection is that I hadn't felt too good. Shall we say, my tummy was a little bit upset. Nothing urgent, if you get my meaning, just a feeling that a couple of slices of toast and perhaps a cup of tea may replace the bacon, liver and mushroom sarnie and a taste of the local ales available to the travelling fan.

The first half wasn't great; we were 2-0 down in the first 45 minutes on what I recall being a fairly bleak October day. Michael Boulding played for us that day and wasn't having the best of games. I considered the option of a trip to the loo before the end of the first half and when I got down there I found the dreaded blue plastic cubicles that look a bit like Dr Who's Tardis. Clearly others had the same idea as they already looked like something from Glastonbury on the third and final day. I decided to grin and bear it for a while. When it got 15 minutes or so into the second half, I knew I could no longer hang on. I dashed to the Portaloo and slammed the door. I had just taken my seat on the throne when I heard the first roar go up. This, it turned out, was Michael Brown slotting home our first goal. At this point I didn't care; there was no way I was going anywhere quick.

History shows that Boulding was subbed for Carl Asaba just before I disappeared. I had stayed long enough to quickly applaud his appearance before I made Mo Farah seem slow in my escape. As I sat contemplating my unfortunate situation, I heard three further humongous shouts go up as 'Sarbs' netted his first in the 77th minute, followed by two penalties in the 86th and 88th minutes to send us back up north as 4-2 winners. About

180 miles each way and I hadn't seen any of the four goals, or one of Carl's hat-trick - just mostly the inside of a badly cleaned Portaloo. The journey home was OK, though. Imodium is a great thing - worryingly at least four people on the coach had some in their bags! I live near Carl and bump into him quite a lot. He was and is a great lad, and was a decent player for us back then. I just can't think about that hat-trick without remembering my torrid afternoon.

CHAPTER FORTY THREE

FOOTBALL RECORDS

ORIGINALLY PUBLISHED: SEPTEMBER 22, 2018
SHEFFIELD UNITED 3 PRESTON NORTH END 2

The firsts and records around the Blades and our famous home are well documented, to say the least, and quite rightly so. It would be fair to say, also, that the core of success on which we are built tends to have come in the early years, certainly in terms of league titles and FA Cups. That said we have had our times in the sun; the title the other year tasted good didn't it? Definitely one of the sweetest memories of my time on the staff, no doubting that. The fact that the last FA Cup final we have so far played in was in 1936 means that the visual records for our salad days are sparse, compared to some. In fact, 1936 also happened to fall in the middle of a dispute between Wembley and the FA that saw the people who would have filmed the game, such as Pathe, banned from the ground.

The only footage taken of the red and white wizards taking on the Gunners was filmed from a great distance above from a gyrocopter. So far up, in fact, that you cannot even make the team colours out. From 1925, when we last won the competition, I haven't seen any film from that, nor have I from 1915 when we beat Chelsea at Old Trafford in the 'Khaki Cup Final'. No, none from the 1902 final or replay against Southampton but there is a short clip of Foulkes and Co. coming out of the tunnel at Burnden Park in the 1901 FA Cup final replay against Spurs. Again, none of the 1899 final against Derby, but that is probably less surprising.

We were one of the first Football clubs to have a photographer/cinematographer attached to them by the name of Jasper Redfern. That being the case, it is sad that no more footage exists, at least, as far as we know. Records tell of United games being held up at kick-off to allow time to get the huge hand cranked camera off the pitch, along with its tripod, certainly in the semis of 1899. I wonder where it all went? Bramall Lane is the same. Despite the fact that it's the oldest ground of its kind in the world and that such a wide variety of history changing events have taken place on its turf, there is surprisingly little photographic or pictorial evidence of what it looked like prior to about 1890, apart from a very grainy, almost pinhole camera type of shot taken from about where the corner of the South Stand is now looking towards John Street.

I refuse to believe that there were not any taken or, much earlier on, drawn, but where have they all gone? It's like the cricket and latterly football scorecards that a man by the name of Billy Whitham used to sell outside the stadium before a game, until the board of directors cottoned on that they could make a few quid directly by producing a programme. I have only ever seen a half of one of those, and even then it wasn't the half with the Blades XI. It was the visitors, Preston North End. I would love to think that there is an attic somewhere in Sheffield that has a box full of them stashed but the longer it goes on the less chance I suspect this is.

Having said that we can live in hope, I suppose. It would be even better if there was a pile of early Bramall Lane photos tucked in with them, as well as a few reels of film... am I being too greedy now? In later years, you get plenty of footage of big games; much of it was filmed and shown in cinemas as a feature, long before television and, eventually, programmes like Match of the Day came along. This gives you a chance to see fleeting glimpses of some truly great names, in a time before camera and filming technology reached the digital class that we have become accustomed to today.

You have to be quick. I have seen milliseconds of Jimmy Hagan playing for England in a Victory International at Wembley and of players like Jock Dodds doing their magic on a pudding of a pitch. I bet there is pretty extensive film of every FA Cup final from the end of the war onwards, I know that the BBC put a series out that you could buy back in the days of VHS video. If you love football it's a privilege to see history made in my book, even if it's not your team that you are watching. One of my passions is collecting classic vinyl - just ask the missus and she will roll her eyes as it has taken over the house - but one day foraging at a car boot threw up another medium for people being able to enjoy the triumph (or misery) of their team playing in a major cup final that I had never even considered might have existed.

Before the days of a Sky Digital box or even the click of a video recorder, it was possible to buy a long-playing record of the game! For 50 pence apiece, I can drop the needle in the groove and relive the splendour of the 1975 League Cup Final between Villa and Norwich or the famous 1976 FA Cup final between Manchester United and Southampton. Viva Bobby Stokes and all that!

The media side of things started somewhere, and that involved us too. One of my favourite Blades firsts is the involvement with the first ever game of football to be broadcast on radio, in January 1927. I mean, this really was ground-changing stuff and we were there at the cutting edge. It's also possibly a measure of the stature that we had in the game back then; not just an also-ran team but one that bristled with internationals, finishing strongly in the league each season and doing well in the cup. Our opponents that day were a club that has also done quite well for itself over the years, in Arsenal.

The match was at Highbury and although a live sports broadcast had been trialled the week before for a rugby union international at Twickenham, and was considered by all to be a great success, this was the first time it had been done with the beautiful game. As Highbury wasn't that far from the BBC's then HQ and the two teams were big ones, the game got the nod and an estimated two million listeners became a part of history. One commentator gave the run of play whilst another spoke over him with just the words 1-2-3-4-5-6-7-8 etc - which only really made sense if you had a copy of that week's Radio Times. That had a diagram of the Arsenal Stadium with the pitch numbered in eight sections, four in each half. Numbers 1-2-3-4 would inform the listener where the ball was in play when the Blades were defending and when they broke out over the halfway line 5-6-7-8 told the public where the ball was in relation to the opponent's goal. This is also where the saying 'back to square one' came from – history was written in more ways than one that day.

Technology has changed beyond belief in recent years. I wonder if any of those who tuned in that day ever thought they would be able to see a game on a small box in their living room, let alone buy it on vinyl to sit with their Beatles and Abba favourites? We may not have the same sized trophy cabinet as some of the others, but this club has played a part in some major changes – no one can deny that.

CHAPTER FORTY FOUR

SIGN HERE

ORIGINALLY PUBLISHED: JANUARY 12, 2019
SHEFFIELD UNITED 1 QUEENS PARK RANGERS 0

The quest for autographs is nothing new. These days, in fairness, the amount of signed United memorabilia that's out there is incredible - just have a look on eBay and you will see what I mean. There is, quite literally, pages of the stuff. When I first started at Bramall Lane, on a matchday you would have loads of kids waiting patiently for the players to arrive in the car park with their books and programmes, hoping to get their heroes to put their monikers on it; a souvenir immortalised in biro forever.

As a kid, I used to come down and do bits and bats on a matchday to help and, as a result, got a matchday pass to get me in and out. When I say pass, it was hardly the kind that we have today - they are like something you would have to get into the Pentagon compared to what I had. Literally a piece of card with 'Sheffield United Football Club Matchday Pass' on it in red! One day I happened across John MacPhail in the car park, now he was and is one of my Blades heroes from that time. I asked him sheepishly if he would oblige, and then realised that all I had to offer was my precious pass. He duly obliged and it spent the next 20 years in the back of my wallet. No real reason, just a happy memory of meeting a player that I admired and remembering how nice he was to a young 'un.

Sadly, in recent years the signing of stuff hasn't been for such reasons. Yes, you will still have the kids out there and quite rightly so, although the selfie has now become just as important, but for every one of them there are others with shirts ready stretched (and very professionally it has to be said). Once is fine, I can understand that; they just want to get it nice for young Johnny or Jenny as a surprise.

Twice and above often, for me, spells out that they have a good chance of landing on eBay in the hope of a nice little profit, and that has other effects. At one time, when we gave a signed ball or shirt over to one of our nominated charities for fundraising, they commanded a decent amount for the group concerned for a raffle or charity auction.

The number around now badly damages that, to say the least. I once saw Phil Jagielka tapped for a shirt by a bloke in the car park, who said it was for his lad as he was his favourite player. Jags being Jags agreed and told him to meet him there the following week and he would sort one out. He was as good as his word and, a week later, he gave him his white away shirt - the one with HFS Loans on the front, I think it was. He handed it over and obliged with a picture doing it, bless him. I know all of this because it appeared for sale on eBay that very night!

The earliest Blades player autograph I have ever seen is that of arguably our greatest ever captain, Ernest 'Nudger' Needham. These days, unless you have a player put their number next to their work it can be hard to decipher just who it is. The new marker pens bleed on fabrics and can smudge on all else. The Needham one is beautiful. On a picture of himself resplendent in his United kit, it bears the legend 'Yours faithfully, Ernest Needham' – perfect handwriting and clearly done in fountain pen. The picture came from his family so that would explain possibly why it existed, and there is a point. You don't see many 'fan' ones from way back and I suspect that is probably down to the fact it was a trifle difficult to carry a bottle of ink everywhere you went!

You tend to start seeing a few more as the 1920s pass. Another great captain, Billy Gillespie, left in his effects a superb autograph book that he took to every new ground he visited as a player, he would then get the opposition to sign. The centre pages were brilliant - one side was Sheffield United and the other Cardiff City and they were done in the dressing rooms on 25th April 1925 at Wembley Stadium, prior to us beating them

A first-day cover, signed by Jimmy Hagan... or maybe not!

in the FA Cup final. He took it around the opposition an hour or so before kick-off. Imagine that – one of the most feared and respected tacticians in the game at that time appearing and asking you to give your autograph in the lead up to the start of the game!

It was some book, I can tell you. The greatest names of the era at every turn of the page, a true "Who's Who" of 1920s English football and all of the greatest and most powerful teams for the world to see. It fetched a small fortune when it was placed up for auction a few years ago and it is no surprise at all. The beginning of the era of writing to a player at the club and asking them to oblige seems to have kicked in around the time of the arrival of one of our greatest ever players, the one and only Jimmy Hagan, just prior to the start of the Second World War.

Now it would be pretty fair to say that, soon after his arrival from Derby County, Sir Jim became one of the brightest stars in football. My Dad loved Tony Currie years later, but if you pushed him he would concede that Hagan was his all-time favourite, he would wax lyrically about every flick and turn that football genius had. The real tragedy was the fact that war took away many of his best years that would have been spent in league football, and he played right to the late 50s don't forget. A key member of the side that gained promotion in 1939 and also of the team that sat pretty at the top of the league when war was declared, and normal football abandoned, his main domestic honour was a Second Division championship medal in 1953 (they didn't hand out a gong when the lads lifted the Wartime League Division North title in 1945).

Although he also played in virtually every wartime England game, they didn't count as a full international game, so no caps were awarded - just an illuminated scroll that sat on a wall in a frame. Many agree that it was a crime that the Blades maestro got only one full cap and it was not only the Lane faithful that rated him highly - the game in general did as well.

His son David told me that this meant there was a steady stream of requests from all over the globe for his signature. So many in fact that in between running a very successful foot-ball career and also a business with colleague Harold Brook on London Road, he didn't always have the time to satisfy all who asked. As a result, his wife Irene, close family friend Molly An-sell, and Hagan Jr. himself all mastered totally accurate forger-ies that could be called upon at the drop of a hat if needed! I would hate to think that a treasured Hagan could be a fake...or any other for that matter, but who knows?!

CHAPTER FORTY FIVE

PAY AS YOU GO

ORIGINALLY PUBLISHED OCTOBER 23, 2018
SHEFFIELD UNITED 1 STOKE CITY 1

I started work, part-time, at the age of 14. Mum had suddenly been left a widow and, at an age when she really should have been concentrating on putting her feet up and taking it a little bit easier, necessity saw her having as many as four cleaning jobs at a time to try and replace the huge hole that Dad's death had left us in financially. Tough times. Her main job was cleaning at the Old Queen's Head on Pond Street and she was there for about 20 years, becoming part of the fittings and fixtures, every morning seven days a week.

The pub is still there, although it got criminally modernised a few years ago, I will never know how they got away with what they did. In my opinion, it really killed what a fascinating building it was (and still is) – my big brother ran the football team there and Dad had also worked behind the bar to earn a few extra quid, so it was a real family affair at one time. One of the oldest buildings in Sheffield, it is also reputed to be one of the most haunted (no jokes about spirits, folks) and I well recall a Sheffield Star team turning up to do a feature on the alleged apparition of an old man who used to appear in the tap room. They put half a pint of beer on a table and persuaded mother to stand looking at it, hoover in hand and scratching her head in bemusement.

She described it as being 'bloody silly'. It appeared in a book on Sheffield ghost stories after being in the paper and it was ironic that, a few years ago after she died, it appeared again in a retro supplement. It was me who got the shock when I opened it! I would do anything to earn a bit of money whilst still at

school, generally used for feeding the addiction of watching the Blades and also to spend on clothes and records. I also gave Mum a cut towards helping with my keep.

My first apprenticeship paid me the princely sum of £28 per week, of which I gave Mum a tenner for my upkeep. It sounds almost Victorian, but I had more than enough to live on and even managed a couple of nights out a week on the proceeds. It's only 35 years ago but it seems like an age now. Things must have been a lot cheaper back then. I remember when they used to have a Magnet night every other Thursday at the Royal Oak at Intake – 50p a pint and that really did make your money stretch. Yes, I did manage a gallon of it a couple of times but paid for it after!

Footballers of that time have told me what they earned, and its fascinating stuff to say the least. I know one of arguably our greatest ever players that never ever earned more than £100 per week, even at the peak of a fantastic career. He always tells me that it wasn't about the money, it was about the fact that he played for a club that he loved and that was all that really counted. When a contract was put on the table he never ever read it, just signed. I bet you that doesn't happen very often these days!

The 1980s were very much the same; a few more mullets and dodgy 'taches present in the United ranks, along with the perk of a sponsored car (complete with name and United badge on the side to make a perfect target for a passing blue and white boot to kick in town). But I know that many of the lads who were my heroes never made millions from kicking a ball in red and white stripes – all have had to earn a living doing a normal day after they hung up their boots. I am not saying that they didn't earn more than Dad did in a factory or uncle did on a building site, just that it was relative, I suppose. The Bassett era lads were, by and large, all the same. Carl Bradshaw, for instance, works in the building trade, as does Mitch Ward. The lads would have commanded more than you or I, but it's a drop in the ocean compared to what you read of the salaries top flight players command today.

A few years ago, I rescued a pile of United ledgers that were about to go in a skip. Hard to believe, but that's what all football clubs used to do with old stuff. Histories just thrown out. There were loads of tales of when the Football League left their famous Lytham offices and what got binned. People were not as switched on back then… just think of what went on the bonfire when you cleared out your Nan's and you will get what I am saying. Hindsight is a wonderful thing.

In the middle of all these fantastic old books was a small leather bound one, actually the smallest of them all, and on the front in gold lettering it says 'Football Wages'. Closer inspection showed that it started on the week beginning 10th November 1893 and it would later prove to be the oldest wages book of the club's in existence. In fact, as far as I am concerned, it is the oldest Sheffield United related book I have seen. There is nothing I have encountered from our birth in March 1889 up to that point. It has been suggested to me that earlier stuff was lodged at the office of our solicitors that was hit by a bomb on the night of The Blitz and lost forever. Slightly more romantic than the thought that it all got binned, I grant you, but lost it is.

The book throws a few important names up. The captain was Billy Hendry back then, and he was on the princely sum of £3.10 per week. Future Blades and England legend Ernest 'Nudger' Needham commanded £2.10, whereas our first England caps, Mick Whitham and Harry Lilley, brought home £2 a piece for their services. Our first 'keeper Charlie Howlett, famed for playing in the net wearing his glasses, was on half of that colossal sum. A few years later Arthur Wharton, goalkeeper and first black professional footballer, got £1.10 for his troubles - still a way above what the working man would have got.

Times and conditions were so different back then - £3 per week in 1893 is equivalent to £370 or thereabouts today - but the cost of living back then bears little resemblance at all. The Victorian era saw an extended period of economic growth, so basically you got more for your buck back then. It's also interesting that the average life expectancy of the working man was around 43 years and the cost of the average funeral £4. The working man would have worked long and hard to take home 24s 4d a week and many earned less than £1 for long hours in bad conditions.

We also know that many of the players had other sources of income - the fact that they earned, even back then, up to four times in some cases the wages of the working man meant that if they were canny they could have a very good living indeed. The great 'Fatty' Foulkes had a shop on Bramall Lane and later a Beer House and shop on Matilda Street in town. Even though by today's standards the sums in the wages book are tiny, back then they were at the very top of the tree for the years they could get out of the game. Maybe, in a way, the life of the footballer hasn't changed all that much. It's all relative, I suppose, but a lot more expensive to watch!

CHAPTER FORTY SIX

NO REPLY FROM ROD!

ORIGINALLY PUBLISHED: DECEMBER 14, 2018
SHEFFIELD UNITED 1 WEST BROMWICH ALBION 2

Great news the other week, wasn't it? Rod the Mod playing Bramall Lane – the first proper music gig on the hallowed turf since Bruce Springsteen brought his 'Tunnel of Love' to the Steel City for two nights in 1988. Now, Bruce has never really been my cup of tea, if I'm honest. I get the whole 'Born to Run' thing, but the 'Born in the USA' stuff didn't really connect with my Dyke Vale soul! I found out by chance, in conversation, that Barry Hubbard, legendary owner of Record Collector and a mate, was actually a promoter on the Boss's first UK gigs in about 1973. Quite a thing to have launched one of the biggest selling artists of all time, and another Sheffield connection, I suppose – either way, the two nights here were a huge success and you could hear it from miles away.

I quite like Rod. Well, the earlier stuff is my thing. The Jeff Beck 'Truth' album is awesome, as is the early Faces and solo stuff. In fact, when you look at his back catalogue it is frightening, and he certainly knows how to put on a show, so it will be one hell of a night that, sadly, I will miss! It has fallen on the same day as Mrs. G's best friend's wedding, and we have both been invited to the whole day. Jane has, in effect, come between me and Rod!

Rod's love of football is legendary and the whole 'Celtic, United' thing sticks out in my mind. I read that he was a Gunners fan when he was growing up around Archway back in the day and working for an undertaker, amongst other jobs. Both our dads had newsagent shops as well, so we would have plenty in common, alongside the footy and music, don't you think? He was also on the books at Brentford and was, by all accounts, pretty decent, playing for the local Hertfordshire Boys side as a centre half and captain before the harmonica and a life on the stage took over.

June next year isn't the first time, however, that the great man could have played Beautiful Down Town Bramall Lane. There was an opportunity that went begging, and that was given to him by none other than club legend and nowadays director and ambassador, Tony Currie, back in 1986. Few Blades who were around that year will ever forget the 'testimonial season' that was put together. The committee hosted various events as you would expect and the late Howard Stephenson was one of the leading lights, along with others such as long-term commercial manager Andy Daykin – the usual golf days, dinners and gatherings that used to make up these years that are seen these days less and less.

The crowning glory was, of course, the gala testimonial game that was scheduled to take place at his spiritual home on 5th October of that year, and what a day that was. For one, The Housemartins played on stage, and they were the flavour of the moment, especially as lead singer Paul Heaton was and is a huge Blade. The 'Showbiz XI' that took on a 'TC XI' was superb, a real tribute to one of our greatest sons.

Woodward, Currie, Colquhoun and all took on some truly stellar names, including Dennis Waterman, Heaton, Billy Bremner and the inimitable George Best, along with a host of others that would eventually swell the gate to near 18,000, one of the biggest gates of the season! As you all know, these games are always purely exhibition stuff, nothing too hard or heavy as a rule and all for the sake of entertainment. That being the case, a host of football-loving names that could put bums on seats and swell the coffers were put together – the obvious one being… Rod Stewart!

Now, I would imagine that there weren't too many people frequenting the Lane Social Club at those committee meetings back then who had a number for Rod, so a plan had to be hatched. TC was, at that point, residing at his mum's in north

TC and Co. in pre-season training

London, and it happened that Rod was playing a huge concert a short distance away at a place called Wembley Stadium. What could be easier? Despatch Tony there to tap the legendary singer up for an afternoon in Sheffield with as many post-match pints of Wards as he could sink and the chance to grace our famous pitch alongside Norman Cook, long before Fatboy Slim was even thought of! I mean, what could be easier?

The date was 5th July and over 60,000 adoring fans made their way to north London to see what was Rod's first ever Wembley date. TC made his way round to the stage door, which I would imagine was the same as the players' entrance. Surprisingly, he found his way blocked by uncooperative security that frequents most gigs. "Can I speak to Rod?" enquired our greatest ever number 10.

"Who are you?" came the reply.

By Tony's own admission, Paddy and Max clearly hadn't got an idea who he was. Quite deflating I would imagine, especially as just a few years before he had been walking through the very same doors as an England player and also the captain of QPR in the FA Cup final. He explained that he was having a testimonial and would like to invite Rod to play in the game. Still no response other than a couple of grunts came forth. Now, Tony is a very humble and, it has to be said, polite human being. He is also not what people expect - far from the flamboyant showman seen on the pitches of the football world. He is quiet and a tad shy if he doesn't really know you. Anticipating that he may not just walk into the green room, he had written a beautifully crafted letter to be delivered by hand, outlining everything and giving every contact number that could be needed. All the info on one page.

Max promised TC that he would, indeed, make sure Rod got it and that TC should wait in anticipation for his reply… Well, a lot has happened over those 32 years, hasn't it? Changes in government, Nelson Mandela was freed, Wembley has changed, Rod has been married a couple of times and we have had a few ups and downs. It would be safe to say that, on 15th June next year, TC will be waiting to ask Rod if he actually ever got that letter, as he never heard another thing!

This could have been his second appearance on the famous pitch, so that's Rod's loss! TC had a great day, as we all did. Joking aside, it should be a top day. Sad, I won't be here to see it as it's another piece of Bramall Lane history that's going to be written, and I would have liked to have seen it for myself. It would be great to have him and TC sing one together for everyone wouldn't it? 'You can do magic' followed by the 'Greasy chip butty'. Just an idea!

CHAPTER FORTY SEVEN

KING OF THE LANE

ORIGINALLY PUBLISHED: NOVEMBER 9, 2018
SHEFFIELD UNITED 0 WEDNESDAY 0

It's funny how, especially when you are young and into football, certain players that you paid your money to watch stick out in your mind many years after others have faded, and for a wide variety of reasons. I'd been attending a fair few seasons in the 1970s, but the first team that you really go both home and away with your mates to watch really cements it for you. Mine was the team that lifted the Fourth Division Championship in such style in 1982. A few of that team remain my heroes.

If ever you could sum up a time in our history, it was the game against the Peterborough United at home that did it for me. As the game neared its end, I turned to my Dad, who stood at the side of me in his usual place on the open end of the Kop near the then fairly new South Stand. He had tears rolling down his face and when I asked him if it was down to happiness at the glorious promotion, he told me he was in tears as he never thought he would see the Blades in Division Four – the older I got the more I understood what he meant.

Ian Porterfield assembled a great team for a fair few quid back then as we all know, and it was a side that really gave the club its self-respect back after a tough few years – any football fan who has been through the mill at times, including our visitors, will know exactly what I mean by that. Keith Edwards was, and still is, my all-time favourite player – I will have seen virtually every appearance that Tony Currie made from my first trip through the turnstiles to the day he left, but I was really too young to appreciate how good he was. Alan Woodward

219

spanned the distance between black and white memories and colour and comes a close second, but Keith, even though a different player to Tony, is still possibly the most natural goalscorer I have ever seen in a red and white shirt, and that's with no disrespect to Billy Sharp.

Tony Kenworthy is up there as is Colin Morris, but I always liked a player who got knuckled in from an early age, and Jeff King fitted that bill perfectly. Jeff was born in Scotland, Fauldhouse, near Edinburgh, to be precise, on 9th November, 1953 – 65 years ago today. Happy birthday, Kingy!

He started out in local football over the border before beginning his professional career with Albion Rovers, making his debut against Stenhousemuir in December 1972. Derby County picked up on his talent and they became his first English club, signed by another famed Scot by the name of Dave Mackay, but he had to wait and make his league debut whilst on loan at Notts County – he spent time at Portsmouth on loan as well before following Mackay to Walsall for a spell.

By his own admission, he could be a "tad difficult" at times. I suspect that being over the border increased the need for a place to 'belong' in terms of how he felt. Wednesday liked what they saw and paid £27,500 to get his signature – he famously played in that derby fixture, took Mick Speight out of the game, and helped the club to promotion as well. By his own admission, he never felt that he truly fitted in S6. His career stalled, he fell very much out of favour with Big Jack Charlton and made repeated transfer requests. After a trial with Hibernian came to nothing, his contract was cancelled and he looked set to drift.

United manager Ian Porterfield had played with him at Hillsborough, as a fellow countryman he understood him and felt he could be a useful player as he worked on getting United promoted. From putting pen to paper on 12th January 1982, he was virtually ever present in the side that flew to promotion and made some truly vital contributions. Few Blades of that era will ever forget the last-minute winner at Crewe.

He was in the side the following season, but what we only know to be personal issues saw his contract apparently cancelled, only to be re-engaged before he scored on his return to the side. It would be short-lived and after a trial at Chesterfield, he drifted into non-league football with Stafford Rangers, Altrincham and Burton Albion, amongst others. He

Jeff King with Kevin Gage and TC

settled in Derby and became a painter and decorator – far away from the sight, sound and colours of a Sheffield derby.

He will always admit that he has had his demons and issues to deal with, and it takes a big character to do that. He is a classic example of the direction a professional footballer can take when the glamour of the game is gone. By the standard of the average working man back then, Kingy earned a good wage from those who employed him, but a fraction of what he would have earned at the same level today.

He would also be the first to admit that, at times, he was not the easiest of people for a manager to deal with, and readily acknowledges this. He made only the relatively modest number of 41 starts for us, with a further two as a sub, weighing in with five goals, but the contribution he made at the time was immeasurable to so many.

The club he always felt that he belonged at was Sheffield United. He will tell you that he identified with the fans and culture. He found a home, at least for a short spell. His prized possession was the medal awarded by the Football League in 1982 as a member of our title-winning side. The thing that meant the most to him, the marker of a time when he was a top-class player – his Curriculum Vitae in a small leather box. At some point, whether simply misplaced or misappropriated by someone who made themselves out to be a 'friend', the man and the medal were parted, never to be together again. The older Jeff has become, the more the medal has symbolised happy times. As simple as that, and completely understandable.

He has always watched games with us, we are the club he comes back to, and I have sorted his tickets out for 20 years. It would be fair to say that, over that time, we have become good friends. A player who was a bit of a hero to me back then became a mate, so much so that he made the journey up a couple of weeks ago to be at my wedding! We have put him in the right direction for some support from the PFA, and they have done a fine job. It was a conversation with them that brought forward the possibility that, in certain circumstances, they would be in a position to authorise a replacement medal.

I worked with them, sending pictures of the ones held in the Legends of the Lane collection to them, along with that of the box. They have changed so much over the years that even they have to be sure what they looked like 36 years ago! The PFA have been stars – tonight, at half-time, we will have the honour of presenting Jeff King with a Football League Division Four winners' medal to remind him of how good a player he was for us. It is an honour and a privilege to do so, especially as today is also his 65th birthday – it's a present from the PFA and the Blades.

We all hope that it brings the memories flooding back and that you keep it safe this time, Jeff. Thanks for the memories, King of the Lane! Many happy returns.

CHAPTER FORTY EIGHT

WHO'S THE BIGGEST BLADE?

ORIGINALLY PUBLISHED: SEPTEMBER 25, 2019
SHEFFIELD UNITED 0 SUNDERLAND 1
AND SEPTEMBER 28, 2019
SHEFFIELD UNITED 0 LIVERPOOL 1

One of the most-asked questions that we get sent to us by email is 'Why does John Garrett look so much like Toby Foster?' The second one is 'Why are you called the Blades?'

There are some long-winded answers, but here is a basic history. You may have heard different or, of course, disagree totally, but this is an easy explanation. Back in the day, and before our Championship neighbours moved to their current abode and the very first Steel City derbies commenced, many of the newspapers referred to both clubs as 'Cutlers' - a direct reference to the famous craftsmen producing their wares in the workshops and forges of Sheffield.

After they left Olive Grove and took their main stand by horse over to a very rural area then known as Owlerton, the same press began to refer to them more and more as the Owls (the area where the stadium sits became known as Hillsborough a little later) whereas we were still known by the original nickname.

This gradually became more and more the Blades, and there is a very straightforward explanation for you. Bertie Blade appeared, we think, around the end of World War One and into the 1920s - a cartoon character that was basically a huge knife in a flat cap. Maybe these days not the best mascot to have for a club, but back in more innocent times perfectly fine.

Via the Sheffield Star you could, at one point, obtain wooden statues of Bertie Blade and Ozzy whats-his-face for a modest sum. You don't often see a pair of them and I'm not sure I would have wanted a pigeon in the house myself, but people did indeed buy them together. We have a couple of Berties in the museum... and very nice they are too.

There has also been a fair bit of history around the club where Blades are concerned. Wardonia were once a famous brand of razor blades and used to be a regular programme sponsor back in the day. They were based opposite the John Street stand in what is known as Chaucer Yard. It's still there and is one of the last surviving 'little mesters' workshops around the stadium, although it is sadly now not in use.

At one point they actually made them there. Latterly they just imported blanks and stamped them up with their logo on them. Wardonia was a brand of TW Wards that were based in the Albion Works on Savile Street, a really proud and old Shef-field company that also sadly succumbed to the decline of steel in Sheffield, but largely because of cement. But that's a story for another day.

The other name you shaved with was Laurel and, as we have written before, there was a major Blades connection here. The factory stood on Nursery Street off the Wicker and belonged to Blades director George Lawrence. He funded the open pool in Hathersage and the one that was once in Longley Park and he and his wife also built 12 houses and a school in Bapaume l'École, a French town adopted by Sheffield after it was deci-mated in the Battle of the Somme.

He was killed during the Blitz in December 1940. Seeing Sheffield burning from his Hathersage home and worrying about his staff, he set off to take them food and drink. As they took shelter in the basement the factory took a direct hit and Lawrence, along with nine staff, was killed. Reports said that the factory was hit with such force that steel stored there for work on the razor blades flew across the road and was embed-ded in the church tower opposite, making it look as though it had been decorated with tinsel.

Incidentally, William 'Fatty' Foulke, our legendary goalkeeper, got married at that particular church some years before. Yes, there are plenty of connections, but more recently a big one that I didn't know about came to light.

And when I say big...

Work at the ground ahead of the Premier League season has been extensive, to say the least. We have been adapting and moving to make sure that all is ready for the new season, and it's been some job.

Most areas, particularly under the Tony Currie Stand, are well-used, but others have been, because of the very nature of what they are, just used for storage over the last 40 years.

It's incredible what can turn up. As I mentioned in my notes recently, a lot of stuff was moved under the terracing itself when the old cricket pavilion was pulled down. Old pictures and the likes. What no-one realised back then was that concrete has a tendency of letting water eventually seep through, down the sides and through the cracks. Over a period of what would have been years, these pictures were destroyed.

I had the heartbreaking job of literally shovelling up what was, to all intents and purposes, just mush. Lovely old Yorkshire and Sheffield United CC stuff, gone forever.

Unwanted trophies collected on long-forgotten overseas trips and at friendlies over the years also had a habit of ending up under there. Not just thrown I hasten to add; on shelves and stored safely, but just kind of abandoned. Dust and spiders moved in and it had a tendency down here of looking a bit like Miss Havisham's from Great Expectations. The area is known as Ivy's cupboard as Ivy Wharrie, the one-time laundry lady and long-time club cleaner, used to keep her hoover, mops, buckets, Flash and dusters down there.

Retail have utilised those areas now as stores. These days all secure and watertight, so good to go. This meant clearing out the remnants and finding new homes for them. We have stores in the museum for such things, so it's a lot easier to manage them these days. Now, in a deep, dark recess that even I had not explored in my years here, something highly unusual appeared.

My lad Danny, who works in the shop part-time, rang me

to say that they had found a huge pocket knife, and asked if I wanted it for the museum. Now, the golden rule here is that nothing gets thrown out without me knowing anyway, and the answer to 'do you want this?' is generally always 'yes'. So when I returned to work the following week from holiday, it was there and waiting for me.

It turned out it wasn't a pocket knife at all. What they found was a huge shaving razor. The handle is a dark, ebony wood and although a little dirty, it's in pretty good fettle. How did it get there? Haven't got a clue. All I know is that nobody had ever seen it in the years I have been there. It could have been made as a special item and then presented to the club at some point, I suppose. I have the feeling it could possibly have been made as some sort of window display item.

I can just about recall some of the displays in the old Mappins' showrooms in town, that had those wonderful oversized items of cutlery and bespoke works that used to be to sell their wares. And wonderful they used to be as well.

It could have been made by either Wardonia or Laurel and presented to Sheffield United as a mark of esteem or partnership to sit in a cabinet in the cricket pavilion or boardroom. As there are no marks on the blade or handle, we will probably never know.

I would say that, looking at it, the age is certainly there, as is the style. It's what we would call a cutthroat and will now go on display in the museum, when I have had a chance to get some Duraglit and polish on it. I reckon that it will come up a treat, and it's definitely a thing of interest that links into the legend of the Blades very nicely - for more reasons than one.

I had to smile. There is often a deliberation on social media about who is the biggest Blade. Ladies and gentlemen, there is no competition. This is officially the biggest Blade that I have seen at Bramall Lane, and no mistake!

If anyone sees this and recalls seeing the blade in a long-forgotten programme, or remembers why it was given or by whom, give me a shout. I might even let you have a shave with it!

Every time we do any work at Bramall Lane, another dark recess seems to give up its secrets. One of the summer tasks saw the club shop extended and so builders knocked through a breeze-block wall, into an area no-one had seen for 40 years. As the wall came down and the dust settled, there were two old large cardboard boxes brimming with files and yellowing, musty paper. To someone like me that's interesting enough but at the side of that, also covered in dust, was a large wicker basket with its lid firmly shut.

Over the years most football clubs will admit that, when such paperwork materialised, it tended to get filed under 'B' for 'bin'. You would be amazed at just how much history has been chucked into the nearest skip. When the Football League departed Lytham for Preston, the stories going round were of player paperwork from Victorian times finding itself ditched next to the rubble from the toilet block that had just been knocked down. That's how stuff becomes both rare and collectable.

How much china has been thrown away when Nan died? How many times have you watched Antiques Roadshow only to hear Mum or Dad tell you that they threw three of those away when they last cleared the house?

One day's rubbish can definitely be the next day's gold. I recall a story of a skip outside a house in Dronfield that had a load of pre-First World War Blades programmes thrown in, along with piles of old books and newspapers. In fairness I don't think they were there long but it just shows that some people don't get what they have.

As I say, there is a simple rule here; before you throw it out, make sure I have had a look at what you have found. Simple as that. Thankfully the shop lads did just that with the stuff they found and I am glad they did. The two boxes are nothing special based on what I have trawled through so far - bank statements from the 1970s and 80s should make interesting reading, letters from the league over FA Cup final ticket allocations, and that sort of thing. You can rest assured that, at some point, there will be a couple of Folklore and Fables lurking amongst the dead spiders and decaying pages.

The wicker basket, however, is a totally different bunny. It has some real age to it and it's clearly a case of finding something that was lying around at the time big enough to pile a load of stuff in. Long before you just nipped to Staples and bought a couple of plastic boxes.

The stuff in it is the stuff I love. There seems to be most of the correspondence and plans for the TC Stand [although to certain generations it will always be the South Stand. Or even, after 40 years, 'the new stand'.]

The original tenders are in there for the work, as are the general rules and specifications for what, when it was built, was the last name in everything new and special in the English game of football. When we commissioned the stand it was one of the very best and biggest built up to that point in the game. A really big undertaking, in more ways than one.

There are documents that tell of the board of directors expressing concern to various contractors, for a variety of reasons. John Hassall, one-time chairman, gives the view that, following a site meeting on July 15th, 1974, the contractors had taken advantage of the non-availability of steel [in Sheffield?!] to 'slacken off' their progress on the rest of the contract.

This had become such an issue that the club was actively looking at ways to use the stand for games without a roof. A further document talks of a strike taking place on Wednesday 14th and Thursday 15th May 1975 by the steel erectors, believed to be over the non-payment of agreed bonuses which meant that roof tresses had not been lifted.

They were clearly still trying to get the stand open as it states that the game against Leicester City was a sell-out and the club, as a result, lost several thousand pounds due to stand seats not being available. Don't forget that it didn't open until the first game of the following season. I always thought it took a long time to build, but I had never considered that many of the things that blighted this country in these periods could have played a part.

Now, to the basket. It's in great condition to say it hasn't seen the light of day for so long, but I believe that it has a very important past. It is one of the kit baskets that we used to transport the shirts, shorts, socks and other vital equipment to games. Like I say, it has some age. The fittings are brass with leather fastenings, and it even has the remnants of a British Caledonian Airways luggage tag still attached to it.

Just think of the story it could tell. I reckon that it could have held the kit of players from before the Second World War, right up to the time when it was loaded with documents and possibly stored away, initially in the cricket pavilion.

A simple wicker basket that could have held the shirts of Hagan, Brook, Hodgkinson, Badger, Currie, and many more over decades... incredible. By the looks of it the basket may have been loaded onto a train in April 1936 to make its way to Wembley for the FA Cup final. It could have flown from RAF Finningley in 1946 as United became the first club to play on German soil after their surrender.

It could have gone to Leeds, Birmingham and Nottingham as the Blades fought it out with Leicester for a place in the FA Cup final and it could have been carried by the players from Salford Quays to Old Trafford when they had to abandon the coach and walk to the ground for THAT game, which saw us top of the old Division One in 1971 and George Best score THAT goal.

The information it has kept safe and dry for years is interesting. What the basket itself could have seen in its working life is truly incredible. When I have worked through the paperwork, it will have a sympathetic clean and then go on display in the museum, where it richly deserves to be. It has survived to help tell another tale of our past.

CHAPTER FORTY NINE

JOIN THE POOL QUEUE...

ORIGINALLY PUBLISHED: SEPTEMBER 14, 2019
SHEFFIELD UNITED 0 SOUTHAMPTON 1

When you work in football you really have to time your holidays. Because of the way they are structured now, the first time I can generally get away is the first two weeks of July, and that's not always possible because of the build up to the start of the forthcoming season. But then that's how it is and you just have to crack on with it. Football weighs heavy on the lives of football staff. For instance, when I got married last year we had to look at when the international break was to make sure we could tie the knot and avoid missing vital games.

We sorted it for the October gap and did it all down at Bramall Lane. Civil service in the boardroom, blessing for family and a few friends in the museum, wedding pictures on the pitch and then the evening do next door in the hotel. Good job Mrs. G is a Blade and season ticket holder, I suppose! Mind you, talk about a busman's holiday. I actually sat at my desk and answered a couple of emails when we were waiting for guests to arrive. And they say that romance isn't dead...

I think I am also possibly the only person to get a Morris 1000 at the side of the famous playing surface in the history of the ground. Sarah thinks more of the bloody car than me and it served as wedding car and honeymoon escape vehicle for the day, so I suppose it was right and proper that 'Geoff' featured in the wedding album as well.

We saved him from the scrap yard because Mrs. G felt 'sorry' for 'him'. I pointed out that it was a car and not a dog, but that fell on stony ground. Incidentally, 'he' is called Geoff because he was first registered in 1966 when, of course, Geoff Hurst became the first (and only so far) player to score a hat-trick in a World Cup final. I wanted to call him Nobby, but....

Anyway, the holiday of 2019... We flew to sunny Mallorca from not so sunny Birmingham. Even though we weren't flying until six o'clock I decided that it made sense to leave our house in Sheffield at 12. Now, as we all know, Sheffield to Brum can take either three hours depending on traffic, road works etc, or one. Today, of course, it took one and by 2pm, we had car parked, checked in... the works. As a result, we were sat in one of the most expensive bars known to man drinking the worst beer I have sampled since Romeo and Juliet's, playing my favourite sport of people watching.

I suppose the tracksuits were a giveaway. Well, that and the fact that they had names on the back but, as I stared over, I thought 'I know him'. I realised that it was our former player and now Swansea head of football Leon Britton. That and the fact that he waved and shouted "Now then Johnny G" – I suppose all three were a kind of giveaway.

That was Mrs. G dumped for a good half an hour as we had a catch up. I always liked and got on with Britts and, despite the fact he wasn't here long (and went back to Swansea) he loved the place and has kept in touch. He is a legend down there and now has an important job, working with another former Blades employee in Trevor Birch, as the go-between between the boardroom and manager. Oh, and Oli McBurnie was around as well...

I gathered Sarah was bored when she laid on top of the cases and went to sleep! The flight out was like me - short and sweet. We also had a result and were the third drop on the transfer instead of the normal very last. As the coach drove off, we both wondered why the place was in total darkness. Have you ever seen the Only Fools episode when they must find a guest house after the Jolly Boys' outing to Margate? Well, here was the Spanish version.

It was 100 degrees, I was melting, it turns out there was no air-con. Not the best news for a short fat lad in foreign climbs. Still, we could hire a fan, but not until the following morning - along with the safe. I would have been too hot to chase a burglar so they would have been well away. After I pointed out that it was too hot, our host suggested we could either:

- Have a swim (difficult as the pool was in total darkness)
- Have a shower
- Sleep in the bath

All good stuff for TripAdvisor, I suppose. It would be fair to say that we didn't sleep too well that night. We didn't get a fan until about 11am the following day - and it was pretty useless. All it did was circulate the stifling hot air; it was like attacking soup with a Flymo. It was black and wheezed, so we named him Darth Vader.

On a lighter note, the rooms and hotel were spotless and the pool was top notch - plenty of sunbeds and umbrellas at any time of the day and, above all, it was peace and quiet. It was mostly couples around the same age and all very friendly, it has to be said. The pool became a perfect refuge after a few hours on the beach or out exploring.

Now, the golden rule when you work in football is never, ever tell anyone what it is you do for a living or for who. It's nice to have a break from a job that can be, especially for a fan, seven days a week, 24 hours a day. No-one knowing you can be bliss, and I mean that.

We had been out for the evening and called for a beer at the bar next door. I wanted to move in there as they had the best air con going. It can offend some when you walk in a place, take your shirt off, and stand under the airstream, but not here. The guy had owned it for 24 years, knew the issues next door and thought it was funny. Well, I think that's what he was laughing at!

An older couple were sat having a beer. Clearly, they had just landed and were having that relaxing, post-travel bevvy. We got talking to them. The usual polite stuff and nothing more. The lady informed us that it was the first holiday they had gone on without her other half's mother for a while - as she was now 102. It was getting too much for her.

Oh, and she was a huge Blade who, despite failing eyesight,

listened to every game on the radio. Wait, where did that come from? I hadn't mentioned either the Blades or the Steel City at any point.

"You are Blades, aren't you?" she asked. "Not the, you know, others?"

Now she had already told me they were from Stevenage. What was occurring here? It turned out that the mother-in-law and her late husband were from Tinsley originally and had gone down south for work a lifetime before. Both sons were born here and the one who was still bothered had a season ticket and travelled up for every home game from the Smoke, despite being in his 70s.

After a bit more digging it turned out that I had come across her mother-in-law, via her sister-in-law who had written to me when she passed 100. As a treat I had asked Chris Wilder to drop her a line wishing her a happy centenary in the year that we racked up 100 points and a league title. I did what I don't usually do and came clean as to what I did and, of course, she remembered the letter and how happy it had made the old lass.

To add to that, her Balham brother-in-law was landing there the next day. He made a point of coming and shaking my hand. He also said that he liked the programme pieces down the years and also had all my books, so clearly a man of great taste and reading! The last couple of days, when we went down to the pool, we had some great chats. I admire anyone who can keep that level of support for the mighty Blades up over all those years and distance, all really because dad was a fan. Brilliant. I also loved to hear the tales of his United-loving 102-year-old mum who tunes in to every commentary and phones David after every game to go through it all.

Usually I would be John and work in a call centre. On this occasion I was delighted to be John Garrett who works for Sheffield United FC, to find out how much the club meant to them. No need to join the pool queue on this occasion. I was more than happy to be there!

CHAPTER FIFTY

I WANT TO HOLD YOUR HAND

ORIGINALLY PUBLISHED: AUGUST 27, 2019
SHEFFIELD UNITED 2 BLACKBURN ROVERS 1

I must confess, over the years I have watched Match of the Day less and less. I suppose it's because we have had, up to this season, no part to play in it for over a decade. In fact, by and large the Premier League had been something that I had kind of decided had little or no interest to me. My club is, and always has been Sheffield United FC, and the fact that Quest finally managed to get the mix right with Colin Murray meant that my interest lay square in the lap of the EFL on a Saturday evening.

That, of course, has now changed. I couldn't wait to get home on Sunday evening after the Crystal Palace game to watch MOTD2, and I suspect that every Blade was very much the same. Yup, I got a chill when the graphics with the club badge appeared even though I had tuned in the night before and seen them already. But little compared to the short film that Sean Bean had done the voiceover for. Then it felt like we had really arrived and made the hairs on this staff member's neck stand up, even though I have heard those dulcet South Yorkshire tones many times before.

I know Sean fairly well. I lived for many years not too far away from the Bean family home in Handsworth, and we still share a good many mutual friends. As a result, I have found myself in his drinking company on countless occasions and used to hook up with him down in the smoke when the Blades were playing that way. He is what it says on the tin - a proper Blade and a good lad to boot. With Sean you definitely get what you see.

Hearing him reminded me of a fond memory of something

that happened many years ago at Bramall Lane after a game and involving my eldest son in the old Lane Social Club. Both my lads are quite fond of a Bond film, and I am afraid, like many things, that's me to blame. Always loved the suave secret agent. In fact, I always fancied myself in the role… and still do. I suppose the only drawback there is that James Bond has never been an overweight, slightly balding 51-year-old lad from Hackenthorpe. That said, if they ever change their casting criteria, I am still game!

It must be quite a thing for a young lad to find out that one of his dad's mates is a Bond villain. Well, it was for our Liam. Now, bear in mind that he has met him on a number of occasions, but not since sitting down and watching GoldenEye where Beany played a rogue agent trying to off 007. This had now changed his complete take on the man who talked to his Dad in the Turf Tavern and occasionally sat on the settee in his front room.

Sean had been at the game and, knowing I would be heading back home in the car, had asked me for a lift back to his mum's when I had finished. Obviously this was no problem and we arranged to meet in the old Lane Social Club for a beer after before getting off. Liam had, as ever, been to the match with his uncle, and the deal was he would be dropped with me at the end at our office so he could go home with me. As agreed, we went to meet Sean for a bevvy. I got my pint and joined them, along with my lad, at the table to talk over the game. For the record, we had just beaten West Brom 3-0 and Marcelo had got a

Liam Garrett

brace! Liam sat on the back next to Beany and all got nice and comfy. Clearly, he was fascinated as he proceeded to stare the Hollywood idol out. "What's up Liam?" ventured Mr. Sharpe himself.

Liam moved slightly away. "Why did you try to kill James Bond?" he asked.

Sean looked a little taken aback. "I didn't. Well, it wasn't me Liam. It was a character I played, Alec Trevelyan."

My eldest was having none of it. "You are a bad man," he spat. "Why did you want to do that? It's naughty."

Sean laughed out loud, and tried to explain to my five-year-old that, in the same way Dad had a job at Sheffield United, his job was that of an actor and, when he took a part, that's exactly what it was - a job. Even though it was on screen with Pierce Brosnan as a part of arguably one of the biggest film franchises ever.

Liam was having none of it. As far as he was concerned, the man sat next to him in the Bramall Lane Social Club was the rogue agent trying to decrease the demand for Vodka Martini (shaken not stirred) by the number of one, for two-and-a-half hours in the film he had been watching on the telly that very week. The debate between child and actor, much to the amusement of the gathered crowd, raged on. Sean wasn't getting through and, to be fair, Liam was having none of it. The junior Jeremy Paxman wasn't letting Handworth's finest off the hook. After all, he had seen the evidence for himself, and that was good enough.

Either conversation ran out or Liam finally diverted his attention to another large Coke and bag of

Sean Bean in the red and white...

crisps, but the inquisition ended, and the analysis of the afternoon's game once again took centre stage. Either way, he let Sean off the hook! It was a typical Sheffield February evening outside that night. I remember vividly that it was bucketing down as goodbyes were said and we left the club to walk up to the car park to the bay where my gold club Rover was parked.

As coats were fastened for the short stroll, Liam looked up at Sean again. "So, you didn't try and kill James Bond then?"

Sean looked down and sighed with resignation. "No, Liam. As I've tried to tell you, it was just a part in a film. James Bond is alive and well, he'll be in the next film and Pierce Brosnan is definitely still able to go to the pub tonight for a few pints of Guinness."

"You promise me?" replied my son.

"I promise," replied Sean.

"Well, that's alright then," came the reply. "You can hold my hand."

And with that, Sean and Liam set off up the car park, hand-in-hand as Liam rattled away to him, possibly about the Sheffield United history that obsessed him more as a nipper than the assassination techniques of a rogue agent.

We dropped Sean off at home, and he waved us goodbye as he legged it up the drive at his mums to get out of the foul weather. As we pulled away, I asked him if he was happy now. Liam looked across and said: "But he definitely did try and kill him, I saw it..."

I saw Sean up top the following day, and he thought Liam had been hilarious. It had made his day. He gave me a signed poster for our young 'un that said: 'To Liam, best wishes, Sean Bean (Alec Trevelyan) - and I didn't try to kill James!' God knows where it went. Liam doesn't know, and it didn't turn up when we finally left the house a few years ago.

It's a shame; it would have been a great memory, as Liam doesn't recall too much about the incident. Mind you, he denies headbutting Tony Hadley of Spandau Ballet in his gentlemen vegetables at Wembley, but that is another story; maybe for another book...

ABOUT THE AUTHOR

John Garrett is the supporters' liaison officer at Sheffield United, drove the 'Legends of the Lane' project and is more commonly described as 'an encyclopedia of Blades knowledge'. A lifelong Blade, and member of staff at Bramall Lane for over two decades, John began writing his popular and award-winning 'Folklore and Fables' section in United's matchday programme almost 10 years ago. Other books by John include Sheffield United - The Biography (with Gary Armstrong), Folklore and Fables, UTB - In Other Words, and 125 Years of Sheffield United FC.